The Musical Instrument Desk Reference

A Guide to How Band and Orchestral Instruments Work

MICHAEL J. PAGLIARO

SCARECROW PRESS
Lanham · Toronto · Plymouth, UK
2012

Published by Scarecrow Press, Inc.
A wholly owned subsidiary of The Rowman & Littlefield Publishing Group, Inc.
4501 Forbes Boulevard, Suite 200, Lanham, Maryland 20706
www.rowman.com

10 Thornbury Road, Plymouth PL6 7PP, United Kingdom

British Library Cataloguing in Publication Information Available

Library of Congress Cataloging-in-Publication Data

Pagliaro, Michael J.
  The musical instrument desk reference : a guide to how band and orchestral
instruments work / Michael J. Pagliaro.
       p. cm.
  Includes index.
  ISBN 978-0-8108-8270-6 (cloth : alk. paper) — ISBN 978-0-8108-8271-3 (ebook)
  1. Musical instruments. 2. Wind instruments—Construction. 3. Bowed stringed
instruments—Construction. I. Title.
  ML460.P313 2012
  784.192—dc23   2012007244

∞™ The paper used in this publication meets the minimum requirements of
American National Standard for Information Sciences—Permanence of Paper
for Printed Library Materials, ANSI/NISO Z39.48-1992.

Printed in the United States of America

Contents

Foreword

Dr. Michael J. Pagliaro's *The Musical Instrument Desk Reference* appears at a time in the evolution of musical instrument teaching and technology when, by virtue of the changes in the world's economy, a more broad-based knowledge of instruments is required. In order to fill the needs of their personal and school budget requirements, music teachers and technicians must now teach and service a greater variety of instruments. These often include instruments completely foreign to those with which the practitioner might otherwise be most familiar.

Specializing in one instrument can seem a divine aspiration. The world will always need experts in individual instruments. However, their restricted range necessarily limits the need for such individuals, and a complete professional career based on expertise in one instrument is seldom viable. Those who choose to pursue a career in instrumental music have no choice but to expand their horizons to include a general knowledge of the more commonly used instruments. Notwithstanding the distinct advantages offered by specialization, few instrumentalists can survive on such narrow expertise. The trend today is toward a more general practitioner form of professional involvement.

Dr. Pagliaro, a general practitioner with some sixty years of experience, has distilled his extensive knowledge into a concise, reader-friendly document. Throughout the book, the various charts and illustrations successfully underscore the written text, and each chapter begins with a quick start section where the reader can easily glean any information necessary to begin work with a new instrument. That quick start section is then followed by an in-depth discussion of the instrument or its family, allowing users to explore its operation in more detail.

Although other sources for this type of information exist in texts and method books, Dr. Pagliaro's reference resource is the very first to combine all of the essential musical instrument material within a single volume. Without question, it is the *sine qua non* of publications associated with the field of musical instrument study.

Looking back over my thirty-five-year career as a music educator, I only wish at the time I could have had in my possession this most essential book. It is an indispensable resource for music educators and technicians, and should live as a permanent addition in the libraries of educators and students at all academic institutions offering instrumental music and music education degree programs.

Dr. Earl Groner taught instrumental music in the Scarsdale School District of New York for thirty-five years, has served as president of the Westchester County School Music Association in New York, the New York State School Music Association (NYSSMA), and the Eastern Division president of MENC (now NAfME). Dr. Groner is also known for his work as music director and conductor of the Empire State Concert Productions and the Scarsdale Symphony Orchestra.

Preface

This manual provides important information for teachers, students, and technicians who work with musical instruments on which they are *not* accomplished performers.

Instant, easy access is available to a simplified version of basic information common to the needs of the musical instrument practitioner, be he a teacher, teacher in training, technician, or student not proficient in the instrument under study. The operative words here are *easy access*. There will no longer be a need to leaf through lesson books or boot up a computer to Google in the middle of a class or project. Flip a page in the book on your desk and the answer will be there.

The manual is formatted with an Easy-Reference Quick-Start section (the first half of many chapters) to provide users with immediate, easy access to illustrated, clearly and succinctly presented information that may be needed during a lesson or for another immediate need. Basic fingering charts, assembly procedures, playing positions, embouchure hints, and other helpful facts are all instantly available for those dealing with a non-major instrument.

Following the Easy-Reference Quick-Start sections are Expanded In-Depth Study sections, which provide detailed, more extensive discussions on the topics covered in the Quick-Start sections.

It is worth noting that the study of music, like the study of medicine, is both an art and a science. Practitioners will sometimes have different opinions on procedures for practicing their trade. As you read through sections of this manual on which you, the reader, are an authority, you may be in disagreement with matters or procedures stated in the text. Topics such as embouchure, alternate fingering, choice of equipment—and those topics that are not grounded in empirical scientific fact but that have more than one direction or process that has proven to be successful with particular individuals—can be open to challenge. The research used in preparation for writing this manual has directed the author to present such topics from a centrist articulation. The information proffered has been derived from a majority of historical successes in mainstream musical performance and study throughout the ages. There is often more than one way to execute a musical experience. This manual presents the method that is most often used.

To avoid the necessity to look back for information previously mentioned that is relevant to a topic under study, and because the manual can be used for specific references without reading it from cover to cover, some repetition will be present throughout the text.

Chapter 1

Introduction

Quick-Start Notes: Fingering

The traditional introduction to fingering for any instrument usually uses a chart illustrating, in ascending order, all of the fingerings for all the notes in the range of the instrument being studied. In this manual, some fingering charts are written in descending order with illustrated fingering because descending is the natural order by which many instruments—and especially brass instruments—arrive at their sounds. By studying the patterns apparent in the descending order, it is easier to visualize reoccurring fingering patterns for all instruments of the choir under discussion. Understanding these fingering patterns greatly reduces the need to memorize each individual fingering chart.

This manual offers basic fingering charts for the instruments under study. Let it be clearly noted that more extensive charts covering alternate fingerings and trill fingerings for all instruments exist and are available in publications that focus on a specific instrument or that deal with fingering charts alone.

Understanding enhances knowledge. If you know how something works, it is a lot easier to work it. This manual helps practitioners understand the technology of all concert band and orchestral musical instruments commonly in use.

The Anatomy of a Musical Instrument

Musical instruments are devices that have been developed to produce and manipulate sounds. These instruments achieve such a high degree of accuracy that they enable a player to perform an almost infinite variety of musical sounds. Although musical instruments are far from perfect, their inventors, developers, and manufacturers have refined their products so as to challenge the ability of even the most gifted performer.

Musical instruments use three basic operating systems. These are: (1) a sound-generating system, (2) a sound amplification system, and (3) a sound-manipulating or mechanical key system.

1

Sound Production

Sound production systems are different for each category of instrument, and are of five types: three for woodwind instruments, one for brass instruments, and one for non-fretted string instruments.

Woodwind instruments generate sound by using (1) a single reed in conjunction with a mouthpiece (as in a clarinet or saxophone), (2) a double reed (as in an oboe or bassoon), or by using (3) a flat, shelf-like surface positioned to allow a stream of air to undulate over and under the edge of the shelf (as in a flute or recorder).

Brass instruments generate sound by having the player's lips buzz within the confines of (4) a cup-shaped mouthpiece. This process is common to all brass instruments. It should be noted that there are variations in embouchure and buzzing techniques that apply to the different brass instruments. The basic principle, however, is the same in all cases.

Non-fretted string instruments (violins, etc.) generate sound by (5) setting a string into motion (vibration) either by drawing a bow across the string's surface or by plucking the string with the fingers. There are some alternative methods of generating sound from strings but these are specific to producing special effects and are not relevant to this work.

Amplification of Sound

Sounds produced by an instrument alone cannot provide sufficient volume and the timbre necessary to satisfy the musical and aesthetic requirements of the listener. Therefore, a sound amplification system is needed to complement the sound-generating processes.

These sounds require a support system to supply the amplitude necessary for the fundamentals and their overtones to attain the timbre desired. The support system is, in fact, the body of the instrument. It is the design and construction of the support system in conjunction with the sound-generating system that ultimately produce the characteristic sound or timbre of an instrument.

Thus far, a device composed of a sound-producing mechanism coupled with a support system to provide the amplitude and timbre desired for a specific sound effect has been described. This coupled acoustic system (i.e., the sound source and the associated structure or body of the instrument) still cannot provide a musician with the equipment necessary to produce and manipulate sounds with sufficient variety and versatility to perform music.

The coupled device is limited to producing only those sounds that are fundamental to the physical characteristics of the design. Consequently, a brass instrument–type construction would be capable of producing only those pitches that are the product of the player's adjusting her lip tension or embouchure; a woodwind design would produce essentially the same type of result; and a string instrument would produce only those pitches to which the strings are tuned.

It is at this point in the design of an instrument that an additional system is necessary. That system must alter the length of the vibrating column so that the pitches that exist between the fundamentals, namely, the chromatics, can be added to the fundamental or open tones.

Controlling Sound

Sound is controlled through mechanical systems such as valves and slides for brass instruments; tone holes, ring keys, and padded keys for woodwind instruments; and the shortening of strings through the use of fingers of the left hand on the non-fretted string instruments. These systems, added to the basic design of the instrument's body, and joined to a sound source, permit the player to lengthen or shorten the vibrating column of air or string by small degrees. In so doing, the player can produce the pitches that lie between the fundamentals in wind instruments and the tones that exist between the pitches to which the open strings are tuned in the non-fretted string instruments.

As the vibrating column of air or the vibrating string is shortened, the pitch is raised. Conversely, as the vibrating column of air or the vibrating string is lengthened, the pitch is lowered.

In the case of woodwind instruments, the altering devices take the form of holes in the body of the instrument. Some holes are open and some have padded, cup-shaped keys covering them. As the holes are covered, the sound-producing column of air within the instrument becomes longer. If the holes are open, the effective length of the instrument becomes as long as the distance between the sound generator and the first open hole.

Brass instruments have valves or slides that open sections of tubing to lengthen or shorten the vibrating column of air.

On string instruments, the length of the strings is shortened by pressing (stopping) the string to the fingerboard at any given point with the fingers of the left hand.

It is the combination of the sound generator coupled with the body of the instrument and the devices used to alter the length of the vibrating column or string that makes a wind or string instrument capable of producing all of the notes that are within that particular instrument's range.

The Science of Sound

Sound occurs when a force excites vibrations in the atmosphere. These vibrations are projected by a series of compressed and released waves of air pressure. Molecules of air are pushed against each other, acting as a train would when the last car is pushed and each car preceding the last one responds in turn in a chain reaction. Since one single molecule of air cannot travel very far on its own, the molecules must push against each other in order to permit the sound to travel.

When this action and reaction takes place in the air, a wavelike motion produces groupings of molecules positioned in alternating sequences. The first grouping of compressed molecules is referred to as *compression*. The grouping created by the void left behind the compression is in a more open spatial relationship and is called *rarefaction*. It is the combined action of compression and rarefaction that results in one complete cycle (Fig. 1.1).

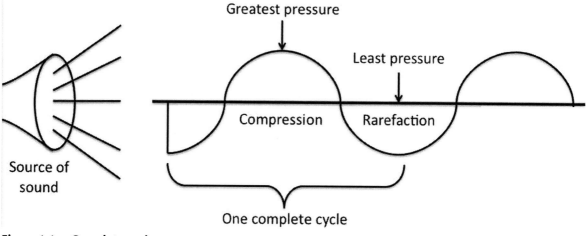

Figure 1.1. Complete cycle.

When vibration is initiated on a string, movement begins at the point of rest or equilibrium (Fig. 1.2, point A). The movement proceeds to its upper limit (point B), begins a return trip traveling back through the original point of rest or equilibrium (point A), and then continues on to the opposite or lower limit (point C). The movement then travels back again returning to the point of equilibrium (point A). This entire voyage completes one cycle. Similarly, one cycle in sound consists of a vibration passing by means of compression and rarefaction through every position that encompasses its point of equilibrium (Fig. 1.2). This type of pure tone is called *sinusoidal* and its image is called a sine wave.

When sound is generated on a musical instrument, the sound presents itself in a symmetrical pattern of vibrations. These vibrations include a fundamental note along with a number of other related notes sounding in lesser degrees of amplitude or volume. The fundamental note alone is a pure tone and can be visualized as a simple wave, free from any accompanying vibrations or tones (Fig. 1.3).

Figure 1.3. Sine wave.

Pure tones are best produced electronically and are generally considered to be musically uninteresting. When a tone is generated on a musical instrument, it is almost always accompanied by a series of related sounds or tones

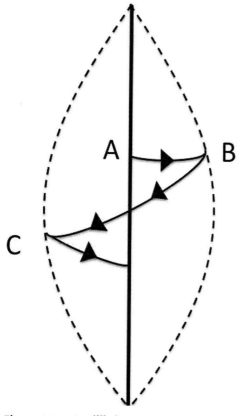

Figure 1.2. Equilibrium.

called harmonics, overtones, or upper partials. These three terms can be used interchangeably.

Harmonics (overtones, upper partials) are secondary vibrations occurring concurrently with the fundamental tone and consist of successive multiples of the whole vibrating body. The segments occur, for example, as one half, one third, or one quarter of the original vibrating column and sound with less amplitude than the fundamental (Fig. 1.4).

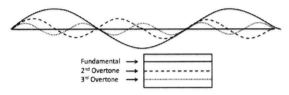

Figure 1.4. Harmonics.

Harmonics are embellishments of the fundamental tone. They are not distinguishable by the listener as entities in themselves but rather serve as ornamentation to the fundamental. As such, harmonics give a distinctive character to a pitch, allowing the listener to distinguish among the different instruments or voices.

Vibrations per second are commonly referred to as cycles per second (cps) or Hertz (Hz), named after the physicist Heinrich Hertz. The number of Hz refers to a number of complete cycles per second, and so 30 Hz means 30 cycles per second. Any given tone is the product of the number of vibrations or cycles that occur per second, for example, "A" 440 is the tone that is produced by a sound generator producing 440 vibrations or cycles per second (Fig. 1.5).

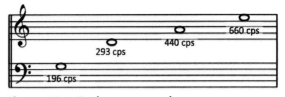

Figure 1.5. Cycles per second.

Although noise is sometimes used in musical performance, tone is more frequently utilized. It is, therefore, necessary to understand those attributes of sound production that modify noise, thereby converting it into a tone. These attributes are pitch, amplitude, and timbre.

Pitch refers to the highness or lowness of tone. The notes of an ascending scale (do, re, mi, fa, sol, la, ti, do) go up in pitch or are successively higher (Fig. 1.6). Conversely, in a descending scale (do, ti, la, sol, fa, mi, re, do), the notes go down in pitch or are successively lower (Fig. 1.7). Any series of notes can take one of only three possible directions in pitch. They can ascend (Fig. 1.8A), descend (Fig. 1.8B), or remain the same (Fig. 1.8C).

Figure 1.6. Ascending scale.

Figure 1.7. Descending scale.

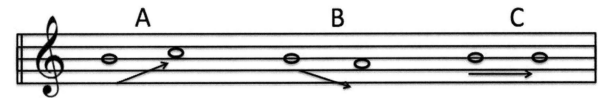

Figure 1.8. Pitch direction.

Amplitude, a form of energy, refers to the volume, or loudness of a sound. Greater amplitude produces louder sounds, whereas less amplitude produces softer sounds. A sine wave is a way of representing a single frequency with no harmonics. If a sine wave is used to measure the amplitude of a tone, the amplitude is indicated by the distance from the point of equilibrium to the outermost limit of the sine curve (Fig. 1.9).

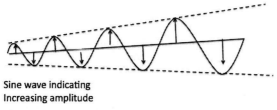

Sine wave indicating
Increasing amplitude

Figure 1.9.   Amplitude.

As is the case with any force, there is a gradual diminution of the energy as it is confronted with resistance such as friction, absorption, or dispersion. With this gradual decline in energy, the tone will dissipate or fade away.

Amplitude (volume) is one of the several physical components that goes into the total character of a musical tone. Amplitude is the force with which the sound is being produced and is commonly referred to as volume or loudness. The more forceful the vibrations per second, the louder the sound. Conversely, the weaker the vibrations per second, the softer the sound. Amplitude does not affect pitch. Any pitch can be produced at any amplitude and, therefore, can sound at any volume.

Timbre is the product of the addition of harmonics to a fundamental sound. These additional sounds referred to as harmonics (overtones or upper partials) (see Fig. 1.4) result from the inherent acoustical characteristics of the sound-producing mechanism (i.e., the instrument producing the sound).

For the note "C," these sounds follow the harmonic sequence pictured in Figure 1.10 and are present in most tones. The same interval pattern would occur for any note.

Figure 1.10.   Harmonic sequence.

The difference in timbre that is sensed by the listener is the result of the strength (volume/amplitude) of the additional sounds (harmonics) and how they relate in volume to the fundamental. The greater the strength, volume, or amplitude of the additional sounds (harmonics) the more intense the nature or timbre of the sound of the instrument. The less the strength/volume/amplitude of the additional sounds (harmonics) the less intense the timbre. An example is the oboe. Tones played on an oboe have strong harmonics/upper partials producing a tone that can be identified as having an intense timbre. Conversely, the flute has a comparatively weak set of harmonics/upper partials and, therefore, produces a more mellow tone.

Woodwind instruments have a series of holes in the body of the instrument, which the player can open or close to lengthen or shorten the vibrating column of air in the instrument.

String instrument players lengthen or shorten the strings by pressing (stopping) the string to the fingerboard at any given point with the fingers of the left hand.

It is the combination of the sound generator coupled with the body of the instrument and the devices used to alter the length of the vibrating column or string that makes a wind or string instrument capable of producing all of the notes that are within that particular instrument's range.

Sound occurs when a force excites vibrations in the atmosphere. When a tone is generated on a musical instrument, it is almost always accompanied by a series of related sounds or tones called harmonics, overtones, or upper partials. These secondary vibrations embellish the fundamental tone, giving it a distinctive sound quality or timbre.

Chapter 2
Woodwind Instruments
Easy-Reference Quick Start

Sound Production

Woodwind instruments share many physical and operational characteristics. They produce sound using:

- a single reed (Fig. 2.1A) held on to a mouthpiece (Fig. 2.1B) by a ligature (Fig. 2.1C) as on a clarinet or saxophone;
- a double reed (Fig. 2.2) as in an oboe, English horn, or bassoon;
- or a flat, shelf-like surface (Fig. 2.3) positioned so as to allow a stream of air to undulate over and under the edge of the shelf as in a flute or recorder.

Figure 2.1. Reed/mouthpiece/ligature.

Figure 2.2. Double reed.

Figure 2.3. Flat shelf.

Intonation/Tuning: General Principles

The axiom is that bigger or longer instruments produce lower sounds and, conversely, smaller or shorter instruments produce higher sounds.

The overall pitch of an instrument can be changed by adjusting its length. However, when tuning by using this process, not all notes adjust proportionately. Some become in tune while others then become out of tune.

This manual will cover tuning at its fundamental level. More advanced tuning procedures for particular notes on instruments is a study that requires the attention of an expert teacher or experienced performer.

Fingering: General Principles

The traditional introduction to fingering on any instrument usually begins with a series of one-note-at-a-time separate topics accompanied by a fingering chart of all the notes for that instrument. Using this approach, the student rarely realizes that every instrument has a simple, repetitious pattern that, when understood in its totality, significantly facilitates determining fingering for all notes on all the instruments in that choir.

All woodwind instruments are constructed with a basic set of six tone holes on the front of the body of the instrument. These six tone holes are covered by the index, middle, and third finger of each hand (Fig. 2.4A). Tone holes in other locations on the body covered by keys complete the notes on the instrument (Fig. 2.4B).

The fingerings for woodwind instruments are similar for many notes. The flute, oboe, and saxophone are very close, and the clarinet and bassoon also share patterns. An understanding of the patterns can be very helpful in determining fingering for the various instruments without having to resort to a fingering chart. Also helpful is to be aware of and to apply the concept that the effective length (i.e., the vibrating column that produces the sound on an instrument) is as long as the distance between the mouthpiece and the first open hole (Fig. 2.5A). As the holes are covered, the instrument becomes longer and the sound lower (Fig. 2.5B).

Covering the thumb hole (Fig. 2.6A) and then covering the six open holes one at a time in descending order from the top down

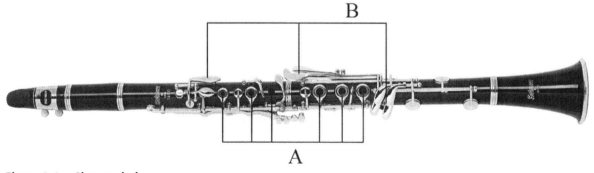

Figure 2.4. Six tone holes.

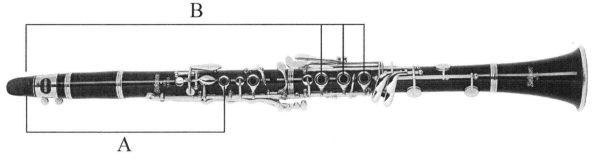

Figure 2.5. Clarinet effective length.

will produce a descending scale. Depressing the register key (Fig. 2.6B) with the thumb hole covered will raise all notes on a clarinet a twelfth. On other woodwind instruments, the thumb key will raise the notes an octave. Pressing the side keys will alter the tones produced when any or all of the six open holes are covered (Fig. 2.7).

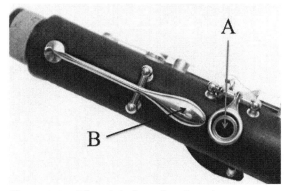

Figure 2.6. Thumb hole and register key.

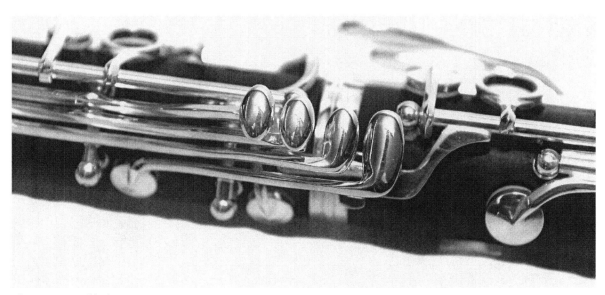

Figure 2.7. Side keys.

Chapter 3
The Flute

Easy-Reference Quick Start

Assembly

The flute (Fig. 3.1) consists of a head joint (A), body (B), and foot joint (C) joined together by tenons that interlock with each other. To assemble a flute, hold the body at the top in your right hand. Do not touch the keys (Fig. 3.2).

Take the head joint with your left hand and gently twist it into the top of the body so that the embouchure hole lines up with the keys. Holding the instrument by the head joint with your left hand, pick up the foot joint with your right hand holding down the two large keys. Twist the foot joint in place so the key rod is centered on the keys on the body (Fig. 3.3).

Figure 3.2.   Assembling the flute.

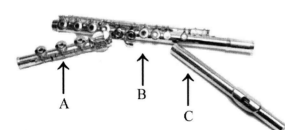

Figure 3.1.   The flute.

Figure 3.3.   The foot joint.

Sound Production: The Head Joint

To produce a sound on a flute, the player rests the lip plate against his chin, just below the lower lip, and directs a stream of air focused across the tone hole (Fig. 3.4). As the stream of air strikes the edge of the embouchure hole opposite the player's lip, the air stream undulates above and below the edge, exciting a pattern of vibrations within the head joint (Fig. 3.5). These vibrations set the air contained within the body of the flute into motion. The body then acts as an amplifier for the sound generated in the head joint.

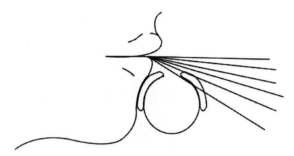

Figure 3.4.   Flute sound production.

Tuning

The flute head joint contains a crown (Fig. 3.6A), screw (3.6B), first metal plate (3.6C), cork (3.6D), and second metal plate (3.6E). Turning this crown will allow you to move this assembly in or out to tune the instrument.

The cleaning rod that comes with a flute has a mark near the end that serves as a guide for tuning. Place that tuning rod in the head joint so the mark on the tuning rod is visible through the embouchure hole (Fig. 3.7).

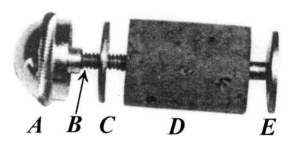

Figure 3.6.   Crown assembly.

Figure 3.7.   Cork adjustment.

Adjust the cork assembly in or out so the cleaning rod mark is in the center of the embouchure hole. The instrument should be in tune. This adjustment is for general tuning.

For a finer adjustment, you can adjust the cork assembly inward to sharpen all notes. However, the lower register will be slightly sharper than its upper octave. Conversely, adjusting the cork assembly out will lower all notes and the higher register will be lowered more than the lower register.

Strive to find the best balance and follow up with moving the head joint slightly in to raise the pitch, or out to lower it.

The Key System

Flutes are constructed with two types of keys: the French, or perforated (open hole), key (Fig. 3.8) and the plateau (closed hole) key

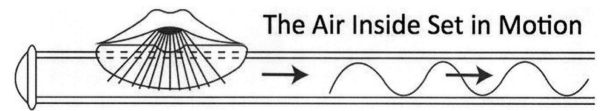

Figure 3.5.   Flute vibrating air stream.

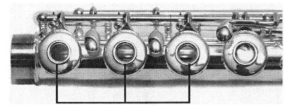

Figure 3.8.   French open hole keys.

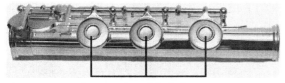

Figure 3.9.   Plateau closed hole keys.

Figure 3.10.   Open key.

Figure 3.11.   Closed key.

(Fig. 3.9). These terms should not be confused with the terms open and closed referring to the tone holes that are open or closed in their original, unaltered position.

An open key refers to a key that, when at rest, is not covering the hole it services (Fig. 3.10). In effect, that hole is open, but it has a key to cover it when necessary. A closed key refers to a key that, when at rest, covers and seals the hole it services (Fig. 3.11).

Both of these keys, when activated, produce the inverse effect that their names imply; in other words, when activated, a closed key opens the hole it services whereas an open key closes the hole it services.

Fingering

All flutes are constructed with tone holes in various parts of the body of the instrument. Six of these tone holes are covered by the

index, middle, and third finger of each hand (Fig. 3.12).

Additional tone holes exist in appropriate locations to complete the notes on the instrument. The additional holes are covered by keys with pads in them and are usually activated by the thumb and pinky finger of each hand.

The flute has many fingerings that are very similar to (if not the same as) the oboe and saxophone. Studying the fingering charts side by side for these instruments will show patterns that will be helpful in determining fingering without having to resort to a fingering chart. Figure 3.13 is a diagram of the concert flute in C key system.

L.H.   R.H.

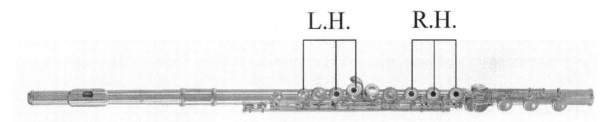

Figure 3.12.   Flute fingering.

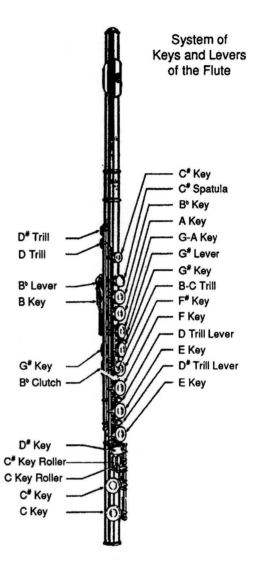

System of Keys and Levers of the Flute

C♯ Key
C♯ Spatula
B♭ Key
A Key
G-A Key
G♯ Lever
G♯ Key
B-C Trill
F♯ Key
F Key
D Trill Lever
E Key
D♯ Trill Lever
E Key

D♯ Trill
D Trill

B♭ Lever
B Key

G♯ Key
B♭ Clutch

D♯ Key
C♯ Key Roller
C Key Roller
C♯ Key
C Key

Figure 3.13.   Flute key system (courtesy of Erick D. Brand, *Band Instrument Repairing Manual*).

The diagram in Figure 3.14 shows the keys of a flute and how they are represented in the flute fingering chart.

Basic Flute Fingering Chart

To finger a particular note, press the filled-in keys or levers in the note, as indicated in Figure 3.15. Low C and C♯ keys are not found on the piccolo.

Expanded In-Depth Study

Some information from previous pages will be repeated for the convenience of the reader.

The Transverse Flute in C

A fully assembled flute (Fig. 3.16) is approximately 26.5 inches (67.3 centimeters) long.

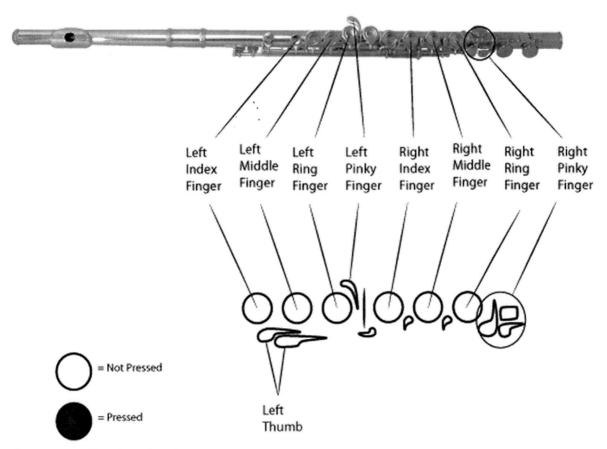

Figure 3.14. Flute fingering diagram.

The head joint of the flute is a slightly tapered tube containing a lip plate into which a tone hole is bored. The tube is stopped at one end with a crown assembly consisting of a crown (A), screw (B), first metal plate (C), cork (D), and second metal plate (E) (Fig. 3.17).

The head joint added to the body and foot joint of the flute form a cylinder or tube in which there are a number of side holes or tone holes that can be opened or closed by key mechanisms (Fig. 3.18).

The column of air within the body of the instrument is set into motion by the player blowing a stream of air across the embouchure hole. That column of air will vibrate to the point where the first opening occurs (Fig. 3.19). At that point, the motion is interrupted and the vibrating air column ends.

The length of the vibrating column determines the pitch of the tone being produced. The shorter the vibrating air column the higher the pitch; the longer the vibrating air column the lower the pitch. The performer can shorten or lengthen the effective length of the tube or body of the instrument by opening or closing the side or tone holes.

Sound Production

As stated previously, sound is generated on a flute when the player, resting the lip plate against her chin, just below the lower lip, directs a stream of air across the tone hole (Fig. 3.20).

As the stream of air strikes the edge of the tone hole opposite the player's lip, that air stream undulates above and below the edge,

Figure 3.15. Flute fingering chart.

Figure 3.16.   Assembled flute.

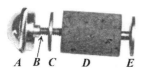

A   B C   D   E

Figure 3.17.   Flute head joint.

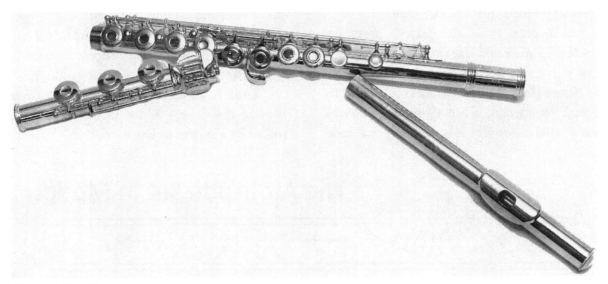

Figure 3.18.   Flute parts.

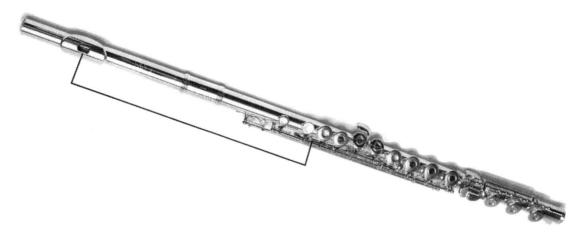

Figure 3.19.   Flute effective length.

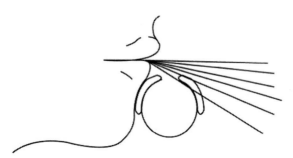

Figure 3.20.   Tone production.

exciting a pattern of vibrations within the head joint (Fig. 3.21). The vibrations within the head joint in turn set the air contained within the body of the flute into motion resulting in a flute sound. A tone produced in this manner is often referred to as an edge tone.

The position of the player's lower lip on the lip plate and the shape of the player's lips in forming a space through which the air is blown (i.e., the embouchure) is critical to sound production. Since all players' mouths are shaped differently, it is necessary that each

individual embouchure be developed as dictated by the player's individual oral structure.

Flute manufacturers are able to control the sound their flute design produces by using different shapes, sizes, and locations for the embouchure hole and the lip plate. The shape of the embouchure hole can be either rectangular with rounded edges or oval.

The sound that is produced by the process described above will only be the sound that is fundamental to the instrument's design. In order to provide the option of producing an assortment of sounds, the instrument must be designed to enable the player to alter the length of the vibrating column at will and with versatility. This alteration is accomplished by a series of holes (Fig. 3.22) that can be opened or closed to lengthen or shorten the vibrating column.

Tone holes are opened or closed by the pads of the fingers or by padded keys controlled by a system of levers.

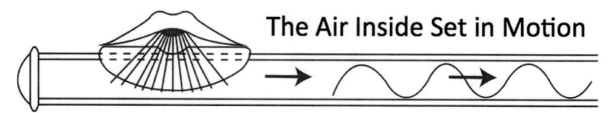

The Air Inside Set in Motion

Figure 3.21.   Air column.

Figure 3.22. Open tone holes.

The Key System

The laws of physics dictate the location and size of the tone holes on the body of a woodwind instrument. Unfortunately, the requirements set by these laws do not coincide with the structure of the human hand, and so in order to fulfill the increasing demand for more notes and greater versatility, mechanical means had to be found to extend the potential span of the fingers. Thus began the introduction of keys for woodwind instruments. Using the modern key system, it is now possible to control the opening and closing of tone holes regardless of their location on the body of an instrument.

Key systems for all woodwind instruments use the same principles of leverage, and are described by the same terminology. The following is a review for the convenience of the reader. See Figure 3.12 for a review of the complete flute key system.

There are two basic types of keys, open and closed. The terms *open* and *closed* are not to be confused with similar terms used to describe the open hole (French, or perforated) keys (Fig. 3.23), or closed hole (plateau) keys of the flute (Fig. 3.24).

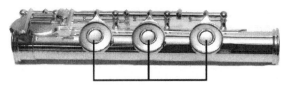

Figure 3.24. Plateau closed hole keys.

Most musicians believe that open hole (French) keys produce a better sound than the closed hole (plateau) keys since the open design strengthens the upper partials of each note, thereby enriching the sound.

The term *open key* (Fig. 3.25), when used in the broadest sense, refers to a key that, when at rest, is not covering the hole it services. With the key at rest, that hole is open, but it has a key to cover it when necessary.

The term *closed key* (Fig. 3.26), again when used in its broadest sense, refers to a key that, when at rest, covers and seals the hole it services. Both types of keys, when activated, produce the inverse effect their names imply; in other words, when activated, a closed key opens the hole it services, whereas an open key closes the hole it services.

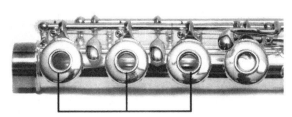

Figure 3.23. French open hole keys.

Figure 3.25. Open key.

Figure 3.26.   Closed key.

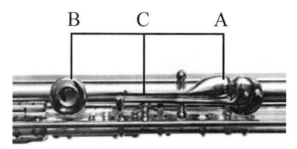

Figure 3.27.   Key parts.

Flute Keys

Flute keys of modern design follow basic principles of leverage using a fulcrum as a pivot point on which the key rocks when activated. There are three parts to a key mechanism (Fig. 3.27). The part in contact with the player's finger is called either the paddle, spatula, or finger (Fig. 3.27A). On the opposite end of the key is the pad cup (Fig. 3.27B). This cup contains a pad, most often made of felt, which is covered with leather, fish skin, or sheepskin. The pad covers the tone hole. The paddle and cup are joined by a stem called an arm (Fig. 3.27C), which in turn is connected to a hollow tube called a hinge tube.

Key Springs

Two types of springs are used to provide the tension required to return a key to its position of rest. These are wire springs (Fig. 3.28) or flat springs (Fig. 3.29). Wire springs, as the name implies, are usually made of an alloy, are

Figure 3.28.   Wire spring.

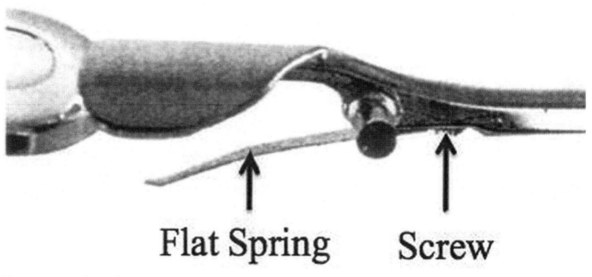

Figure 3.29.   Flat spring.

cut to the length required by its position on the instrument, and are inserted into a hole in the post that holds the flute key in place.

Flat springs are also made of various metal alloys and are shaped and sized to fit their position on the instrument. A flat spring has a hole drilled in the contact end when a screw is inserted to hold the spring on the key.

Tone Holes

Tone holes on flutes and saxophones extend out from the body, whereas on other woodwind instruments, tone holes are usually drilled into the instrument's body. The flute tone hole can be constructed independently of the body and then soldered in place (Fig. 3.30), or it can be drawn from the material of the body itself.

The process used to construct drawn tone holes consists of drilling a small hole in the body of the flute and then pulling a series of balls of increasingly larger size through the hole. The drawing process pulls the material

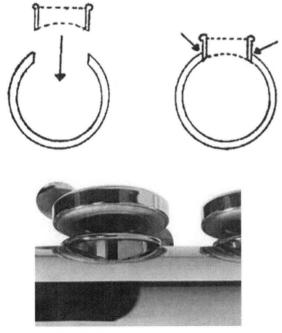

Figure 3.30.   Soldered tone holes.

from the inside of the body upward, forming a cup-like projection that extends from the flute body. The resulting projection is then leveled and its edge is rolled, providing a smoother surface on which the pad can rest. This process creates a smoother extrusion, which is thought by some to produce less resistance to the air flow and therefore a better tone (Fig. 3.31).

Figure 3.31.   Drawn tone holes.

The Flute Family

At this time only four members of the flute family are commonly used in contemporary orchestras. The concert flute in C (Fig. 3.32) is the most common and easily recognizable. This instrument has a prominent role in orchestral, concert band, and marching band repertoires as well as in solo works.

The piccolo in C (Fig. 3.33) is a small version of the C flute, sounding one octave higher than the C flute. Often used to double for the flute and/or violin melodies to add brightness or an "edge" to the sound, the piccolo in C is also used to add an obbligato or decorative upper melody to a selection. This technique can best be heard in some of the more popular marches by John Philip Sousa.

Next in order of descending sound below the C flute is the alto flute in G (Fig. 3.34). This instrument transposes a fourth lower than the written note. However, it maintains the same written range in the score. The alto flute is not particularly effective in the higher

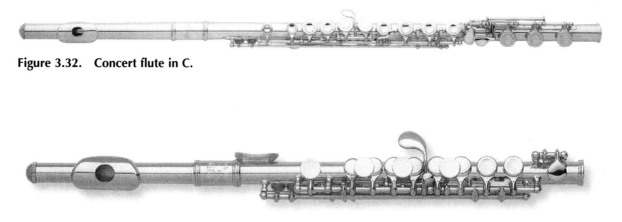

Figure 3.32.   Concert flute in C.

Figure 3.33.   Piccolo in C.

register, but in the middle and lower registers it produces a very mellow, rich tone.

At the lowest end of the range of the flute family is the bass flute in C (Fig. 3.35). This flute sounds an octave lower than the written note while it shares the same written range as the C flute.

Due to the extraordinary size of the instrument and the comparatively large size of the embouchure hole in the head joint, many players have a difficult time adjusting to the bass flute after playing the other instruments of the family. A great deal more airflow is required to generate the vibrations that excite the air column within the body of the instrument. However, the resulting sound is a rich and haunting tone, which is most useful for special effects. Three additional flutes are available but seldom used. These include the following:

- the treble flute in G (Fig. 3.36);
- the soprano in E♭ (Fig. 3.37); and
- the tenor in B♭ (Fig. 3.38).

These instruments are sometimes used for special effects or to satisfy the needs of a particular score.

Figure 3.34.   Alto flute in G.

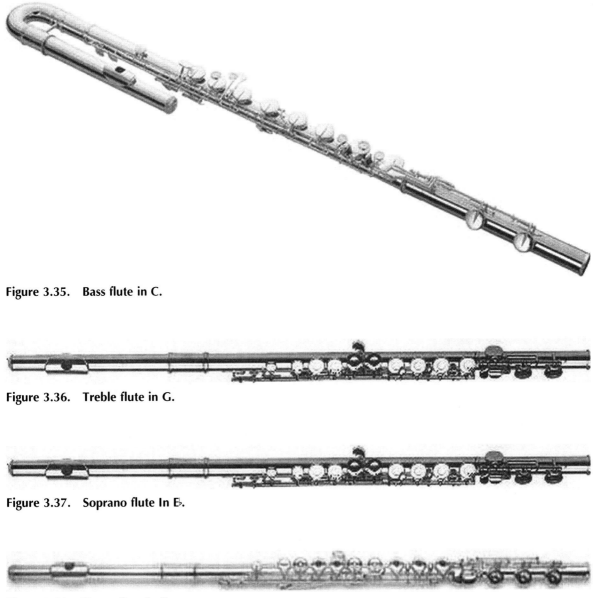

Figure 3.35. Bass flute in C.

Figure 3.36. Treble flute in G.

Figure 3.37. Soprano flute In E♭.

Figure 3.38. Tenor flute in B♭.

Summary

Sound is generated on the flute through the use of an edge-tone, air-reed-type head joint. The sound generated is amplified through the body of the flute and manipulated by a side-hole-shortening keyed system.

Flutes are made of a variety of products ranging from wood through crystal and including numerous metals and alloys. Of greatest importance is the fact that the tone quality of a flute is almost entirely the product of the design of the head joint and body. The material used in the construction of the body and keys of the flute has little effect on its tone quality.

Chapter 4
The Clarinet

Easy-Reference Quick Start

Assembly

The B♭ soprano clarinet (Fig. 4.1) consists of a mouthpiece, ligature (A); barrel (B); upper joint (C); lower joint (D); and bell (E). All of the sections are connected by cork-covered tenons (F), which fit into sockets. The upper and lower joints are fitted with keys in the form of open rings and levers attached to padded keys (G). To assemble a clarinet, follow these steps:

1. Lubricate the tenons with cork grease (F).
2. Grasp the upper joint (C) with your left hand and press down the tone hole rings (G). This will raise the bridge

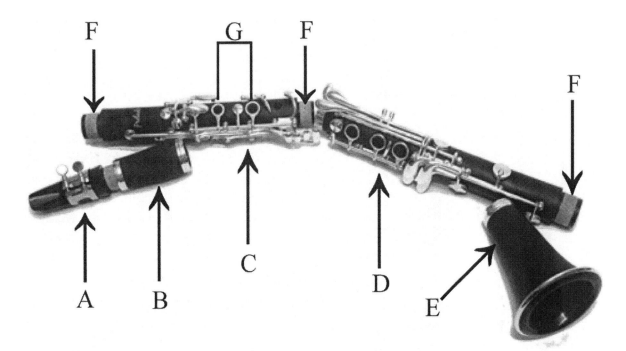

Figure 4.1.   Clarinet parts.

Figure 4.2.   Bridge key.

key (Fig. 4.2) and prevent it from be-ing damaged.

3. Hold the lower joint at the bottom with your right hand, being careful not to bend the rods or keys, and twist the two sections together so that the bridge keys line up.

4. Holding the lower joint in your left hand, twist on the bell.

5. Twist the mouthpiece onto the bar-rel and then twist the barrel onto the upper joint with the flat, reed side of the mouthpiece facing the back of the clarinet.

6. Place the reed (Fig. 4.3A) on the flat side of the mouthpiece (Fig. 4.3B) so that a credit card's thickness of mouthpiece is showing above the tip of the reed.

Figure 4.3.   Reed/mouthpiece/ligature.

7. Place the ligature (Fig. 4.3C) over the reed and mouthpiece to the level of the marking on the mouthpiece. The ligature screws should be on the side of the reed.

8. Tighten the two screws.

Sound Production: Embouchure

The word *embouchure* refers to the position of the lips and facial muscles when playing a wind instrument.

To form a proper embouchure for a clari-net, pull back the lower lip over the lower teeth just enough to form a pad for the teeth. Too much padding will restrict the reed's vibration.

Place the mouthpiece in the mouth with the reed resting on the lower lip at the point of the reed where it gradually slopes away from the flat surface of the mouthpiece. This will allow the reed to vibrate freely to pro-duce a sound.

Figure 4.4 shows a side view of a mouth-piece facing that gradually slopes away from the plane of the table. This configuration allows the reed to vibrate and produce a sound. Another way to see this space is to view the mouthpiece (with a reed in place) from the side with a light behind it. You will easily see the point at which the reed leaves the plane of the mouthpiece. The reed vibrates from that point up. The exact point where the reed contacts the lower lip will be determined by the player's lip size and con-figuration in conjunction with the lower teeth configuration. A bit of trial and error will help locate the sweet spot.

1. Place the upper teeth firmly on top of the mouthpiece.

2. Close the lips around the mouthpiece with a slight smile keeping the corners firm so that no air can escape.

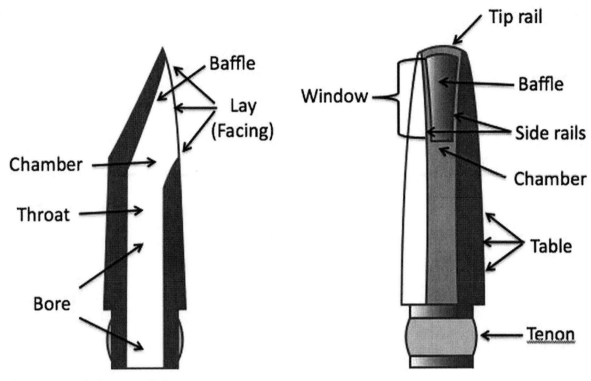

Figure 4.4. Clarinet mouthpiece.

3. Keep the chin muscles firm and pulling down.
4. Hold the clarinet at approximately a thirty-degree angle from the body.
5. Blow gently into the instrument while adjusting it in-out-away-toward the body until a proper clarinet sound is achieved. (When this sound occurs, the player has established his own proper embouchure and playing position.)
6. When playing the clarinet, the tongue should be pointing at the reed but not touching it. The player's cheeks should be firm and not puffed.

Tuning

To tune a clarinet, the most commonly used method is to adjust the barrel in or out of the upper joint. To raise the pitch, gently twist the barrel into the upper joint. To lower the pitch, use the same twisting motion to move the barrel out of the upper joint.

Open "G" (concert "F") is the note usually used for tuning. This is effective for general tuning; however, not all notes on the instrument respond to that process. A more comprehensive tuning can be achieved by using the in-and-out process used on the barrel on the middle joint of the instrument.

Fingering

The clarinet, like the other woodwind instruments, is constructed with a basic set of six tone holes on the front of its body (Fig. 4.5). The six tone holes are covered by the index, middle, and third finger of each hand with the left hand covering the top three holes and the right hand covering the bottom three holes.

Additional tone holes exist in appropriate locations on the body to complete the notes

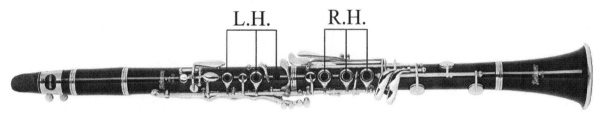

Figure 4.5. Clarinet fingering.

on the instrument. These holes are covered by keys with pads in them and are articulated by the thumb, pinky fingers, and the sides of the index fingers between the first and second knuckle on each hand.

When playing the clarinet, the effective length of the instrument is as long as the distance between the mouthpiece and the first open hole (Fig. 4.6A). As the holes are covered, the effective length of the instrument becomes longer and the sound lower (Fig. 4.6B).

Determining the fingering for a clarinet without a fingering chart can be achieved by covering the thumb hole (Fig. 4.7A) and then covering the six open holes one at a time in descending order from the top down. Adding the side keys will alter the tone produced when any or all of the six open holes are covered.

Unique to the clarinet is a register key (Fig. 4.7B) in place of the octave key found on other woodwind instruments. Engaging the register key raises the pitch on a clarinet a twelfth instead of an octave.

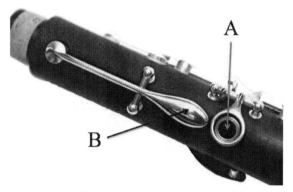

Figure 4.7. Clarinet thumb hole and register key.

There are many fingerings that are very similar, if not the same, for the clarinet and bassoon. Studying the charts for those instruments side by side will show patterns that will be helpful in determining fingering without having to resort to a fingering chart (Fig. 4.8).

Basic Clarinet Fingering Chart

To finger a particular note, cover the filled-in holes and depress the filled-in keys or levers shown in the drawing above the note (Fig. 4.9).

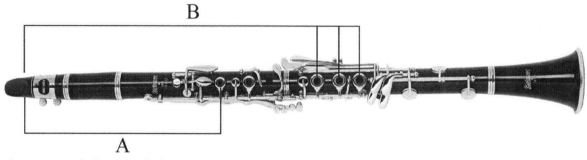

Figure 4.6. Clarinet tone holes.

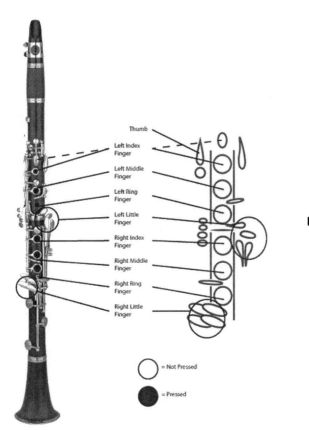

Thumb
Left Index Finger
Left Middle Finger
Left Ring Finger
Left Little Finger
Right Index Finger
Right Middle Finger
Right Ring Finger
Right Little Finger

◯ = Not Pressed

● = Pressed

Figure 4.8. Clarinet fingering diagram.

Expanded In-Depth Study

The Instrument

The clarinet is a single-reed, mostly cylindrical tube about twenty-six inches (sixty-six centimeters) long. The body of the instrument is not totally cylindrical but instead flares out slightly at its lowest segment to accommodate the bell, which continues the flare shape to the end of the instrument. The mouthpiece is tapered toward the tip so that the entire instrument, although cylindrical for the most part, actually starts off small, but ends up larger.

Most B♭ soprano clarinets are designed to disassemble into five parts (Fig. 4.10). These are the mouthpiece (A), barrel (B), upper (C) and lower (D) joints, and the bell (E). The purpose of this segmentation is primarily for convenience in packing and carrying, but it also permits the replacement of a single section rather than the entire instrument, should serious damage occur. All of the joints are connected by cork-covered tenons (F), which fit into sockets.

One of the unique acoustical characteristics of the clarinet is that its sound production emphasizes the odd-numbered overtones as opposed to the more even distribution of overtones present in other woodwind instruments. The result is that sound that is particular to the clarinet.

The playing range of the clarinet is divided into three sections. The lowest range is called the chalameau (low E to mid-B♭); the middle range is the clarion (mid-B natural

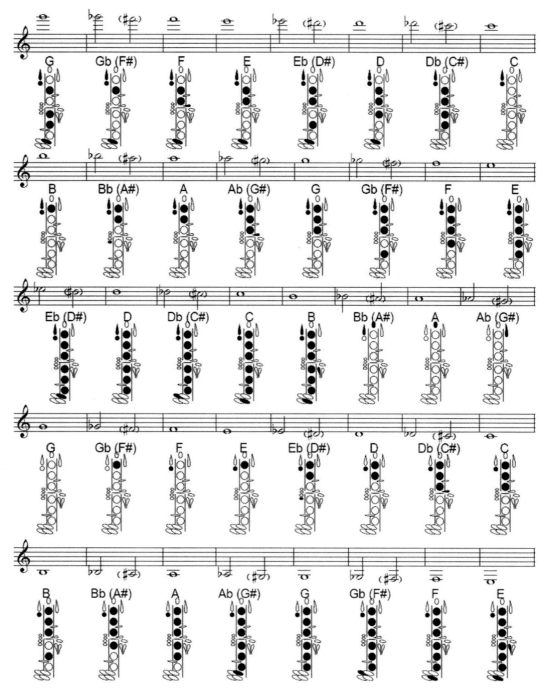

Figure 4.9. Basic clarinet fingering chart.

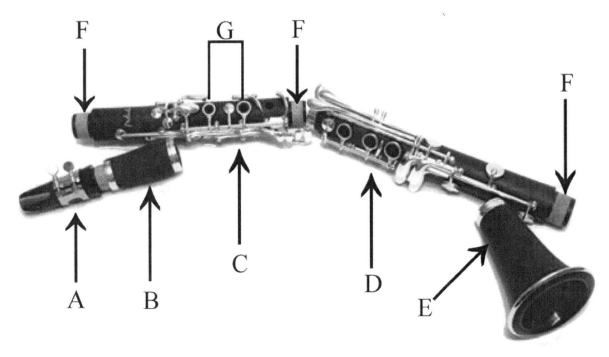

Figure 4.10. Clarinet parts.

to high C); the highest range is the altissimo (extreme or acute register high C and up).

The Key System

The mechanism or key system of the clarinet went through around two centuries of evolution before becoming what is now referred to as the Boehm system (Fig. 4.11), named after Theobald Boehm. However, Boehm had little, if anything, to do with the development and design of the key mechanism. His primary accomplishment was in determining the placement of the tone holes in the body of the instrument so that the laws of acoustics were sufficiently satisfied. The actual mechanism was developed by Klose and Buffet.

Since Boehm's research findings required placement of tone holes that rendered playing with the human hand impossible, Hyacinthe-Eleonore Klose, a teacher of clarinet at the Paris Conservatory, and Louis-Auguste Buffet, still a well-known name in clarinet manu-

facturing, collaborated to invent a key system that would accommodate Boehm's design.

The current Boehm model clarinet has twenty-four tone holes that are controlled by seventeen keys and six rings. These rings are actually open circles of metal that encircle tone holes. When the tone hole is covered by the player's finger, the ring activates a reciprocal action that in turn covers one or more additional holes. A number of modifications have been made on the key system primarily intended to facilitate the player's transition from one note to another, or to produce a trill that may be particularly awkward to execute.

Sound Production:
The Mouthpiece

Sound is generated on the clarinet by means of a single cane reed attached by a ligature to a well-designed and carefully constructed mouthpiece (Fig. 4.12). As a player initiates a stream of air flowing through and against the

Clarinet with Boehm Key System

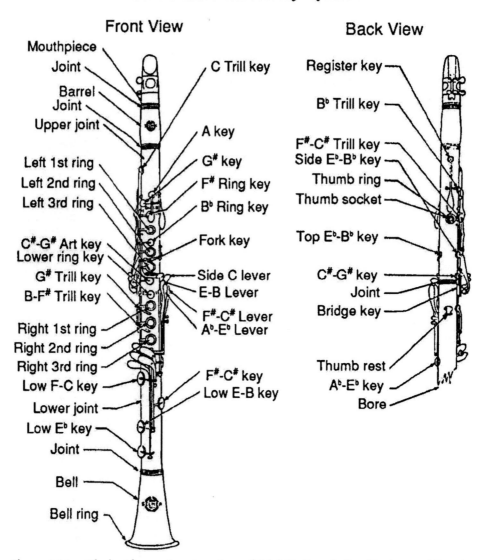

Figure 4.11. Clarinet key system (courtesy of Erick D. Brand, *Band Instrument Repairing Manual*).

Figure 4.12.   Reed/mouthpiece/ligature.

reed/mouthpiece combination, the reed is set in motion, vibrating against the mouthpiece. This excites the column of air within the body of the instrument to vibrate, producing a sound.

Current research in the technology of musical instruments offers voluminous evidence to indicate that the quality of sound produced by woodwind instruments is more

the result of the mouthpiece/reed combination than of any other factor or combination of factors incorporated in the design or construction of the instrument.

Figure 4.13 shows diagrams of the clarinet mouthpiece, indicating the names of the parts. The table is flat and is the point at which the reed makes contact with the mouthpiece. Above the table is the facing. This section, sometimes referred to as the lay, is shaped so that it gradually slopes away from the plane of the table. It is at this point that the reed vibrates against the mouthpiece, generating the initial sound. The trajectory of this slope creates the space the reed has in which to vibrate.

On either side of the facing are side rails. It is absolutely essential that they be identical, neither too wide nor too narrow, and that they have a perfect finish, free of warping or defects of any kind.

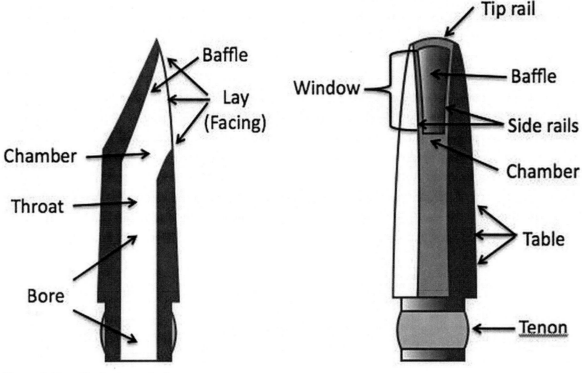

Figure 4.13.   Clarinet mouthpiece.

The tip rail must adhere to the same standards of perfection as the side rails. It is rounded to follow the contour of the reed. This part of the perimeter of the window completes the portion of the mouthpiece that makes a seal with the reed. A tip rail of about one thirty-second of an inch (.8 millimeters) is most effective for general use.

The window is the space between the rails. It channels the vibrations of the reed into the instrument and excites the air column in the instrument to produce the tone. The recommended width of the window at the top is slightly less than half an inch (11.5 millimeters).

The baffle should measure about three-eighths of an inch and be moderately concave in structure, flattening out as it approaches the tip rail.

The bore of the mouthpiece is critical to the tone quality and pitch of the instrument. It is the point where the mouthpiece, carrying the "raw" generated sound, meets the bore of the instrument and begins to become a tone. As such, the bore of the mouthpiece must match the bore of the instrument in order to allow a smooth, uninterrupted surface for the vibrating column of air to travel into the instrument.

Clarinet mouthpieces have been made of practically every material imaginable. However, over the centuries, trial and error have encouraged the industry to settle upon the use of wood, glass, crystal, plastic, or hard rubber. Although the material used is of some consequence, its importance must be judged in conjunction with other design considerations in making a mouthpiece. Among these are the length of the facing or lay and the size of the opening at the tip.

In the broadest terms it could be said that extremes in the design of any aspect of the mouthpiece should be avoided, if the designer is to provide for the average student or player. Conversely, at the top level of professional performance, a highly specialized design can be obtained through the combined efforts of the performer and the mouthpiece maker.

Although there are trends that seem to indicate that certain materials and dimensions are more effective than others for general use, it is important to bear in mind that all recommendations for such designs must be subject to the needs and physical individuality of the player. All rules must allow for exceptions.

The Barrel, Joints, and Bell

The first phase of the voyage of the column of air that has been excited into motion by the sound generator (i.e., mouthpiece and reed) takes place within the barrel of the instrument (Fig. 4.14). The barrel is a short cylindrical section used to join the mouthpiece to the body of the clarinet.

Although the original Boehm patent dispensed with the barrel, making the upper joint one piece, the barrel has remained a part of all instruments to date. There is some rationale to its persisting in that it can function as an aid to tuning. The player can extend or contract

Figure 4.14.   Clarinet barrel.

the overall length of the instrument by moving the barrel slightly in or out of the upper joint, thereby raising or lowering the instrument's overall pitch.

Of equal importance is the fact that the barrel is the first part of the body of the instrument to receive the flow of warm, moist air from the mouthpiece. It is, consequently, subjected to the greatest amount of expansion and contraction from the constant humidity and temperature changes, which often result in cracking the wood. In such a case, a simple replacement of the barrel will resolve the problem as opposed to having to repair or replace the entire upper joint of the instrument.

Following the mouthpiece and barrel, the third and fourth sections of the clarinet are the upper and lower joints. These are essentially cylindrical in shape, though there is some flaring in the lower joint, starting anywhere from the fourth lowest side hole to the last hole. Flaring is necessary to compensate for the acoustical inconsistencies inherent in the clarinet design.

The bell of the clarinet is the lowest portion of the body. This section serves as an extension of the sound amplification system. It also compensates for the absence of subsequent open holes when all holes are closed to play the lowest note on the instrument.

When a note other than the lowest one is played, some side holes are closed with the remainder left open. The last two (or at most three) of these remaining open holes allow the tone to radiate from the instrument, thereby enhancing tone quality and amplification. When the lowest note on the instrument is reached, these successive open amplifying holes no longer exist causing the tone quality and amplification to suffer. The addition of the bell compensates for the absence of the amplifying holes by acting as an extension of the amplification system.

Characteristic Sound

The tone quality or timbre of any instrument is a result of the intensity of the overtones (harmonics or upper partials) of that tone in relation to its fundamental. The quantity and intensity of these overtones superimposed upon the fundamental result in the timbre that is identified with any particular instrument.

In the case of the clarinet, the even-numbered upper partials (i.e., the second, fourth, sixth, etc.) are present in relatively smaller amplitude as compared to the odd-numbered (i.e., the third, fifth, etc.) partials. This imbalance accounts for the characteristic clarinet sound.

Material

The material used in constructing a clarinet has little or no effect on the tone quality. Empirical studies strongly indicate that those involved in the selection of musical instruments—in this case, clarinets—should direct most of their attention to the sound-generating aspect of the outfit while giving less attention to the material from which the body is made.

This conclusion is of particular importance to those who must consider the cost of the instrument they are purchasing. The mouthpiece and reed on the clarinet deserve the greatest investment, while the materials from which the remainder of the instrument is constructed are of less importance.

The Clarinet Family

The inventiveness of the human mind has resulted in the creation of numerous clarinets of assorted sizes and transpositions in order to accommodate the player, or to produce special effects. At this time in our musical evolution, some of the many choices of clarinets commonly in use are A♭ and E♭ sopranino, B♭ soprano, A soprano, F basset horn, E♭ alto, B♭ bass, EE♭ contra-alto, and BB♭ contrabass. Figure 4.15 shows a comparison of the sizes and general shapes of several members of the clarinet family.

For all clarinets, the sound generators, bodies, mechanisms, and acoustical principles are essentially the same. The significant differences are in the size and transposition, and in the shape of the bell and of the coupling devices connecting the mouthpieces to the main bodies of the instruments.

Representatives of the Clarinet Family

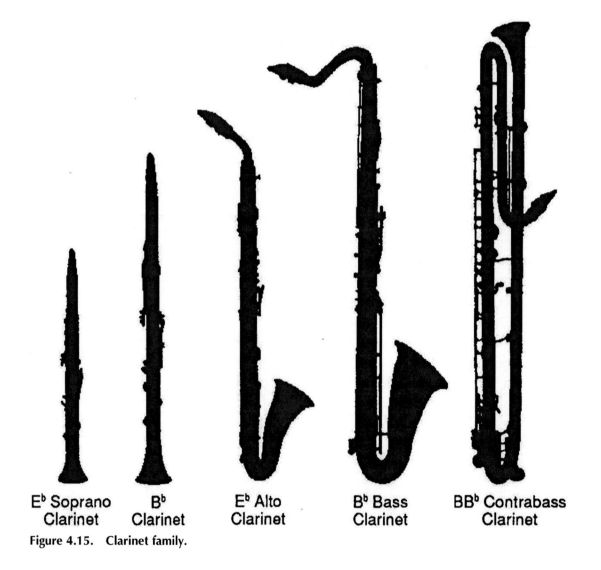

E♭ Soprano Clarinet   B♭ Clarinet   E♭ Alto Clarinet   B♭ Bass Clarinet   BB♭ Contrabass Clarinet

Figure 4.15.   Clarinet family.

Summary

Studies clearly indicate that the essence of the clarinet's sound quality is primarily the product of the mouthpiece and that all that follows serves merely as a means to amplify and manipulate that sound.

The clarinet is an acoustically complex instrument. Its cylindrical design lessens the intensity of the even-numbered upper partials in relation to the fundamental, and emphasizes the odd-numbered partials. Since it functions as a cylinder, as opposed to a cone, the acoustical balance of nodes and anti-nodes (points of interrupted vibration and of greatest vibration) results in the instrument overblowing at the twelfth instead of the octave, as do the other woodwinds. This then increases the complexity of the tone hole placement and size so that accurate intonation relationships among the registers become virtually impossible. The solution is found in placing and sizing the tone holes in such a way that none of the registers is radically out of tune yet never truly in tune.

Although some attempts have been made to alter and improve the shortcomings of the clarinet, change in the music world comes slowly. This tortoise-paced progress is further slowed by the general unwillingness of musicians to accept innovation readily.

Chapter 5

The Saxophone

Easy-Reference Quick Start

The Instrument

The saxophone bridges the gap between the brass and woodwind instruments because it is made of brass but uses a single-reed mouthpiece. The instrument is made in three sections (Fig. 5.1): the mouthpiece (A), neck (B), and body (C).

Assembly

Assembling a saxophone is relatively simple (Fig. 5.2), as shown by the following steps:

1. Insert the neck (A) into the top of the body (B), being careful not to bend the octave key (C).

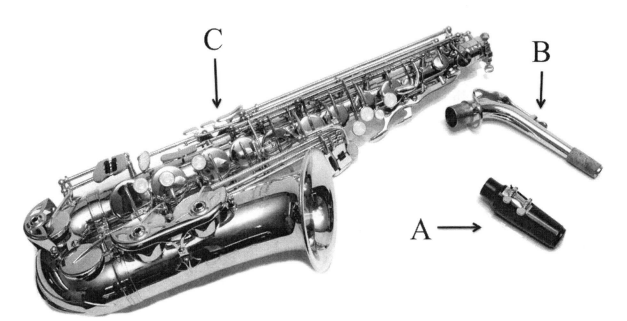

Figure 5.1.   Saxophone parts.

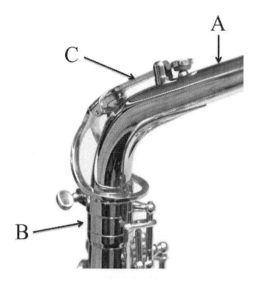

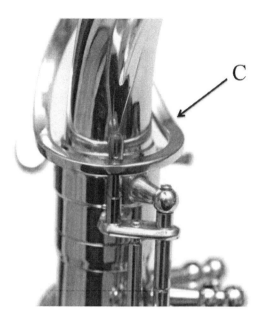

Figure 5.2.   Saxophone octave key.

2. Using a twisting motion, work the mouthpiece onto the neck (Fig. 5.3).

3. After the mouthpiece is on the neck, using Figure 5.4 as your guide, place the reed (A) on the flat side of the mouthpiece (B) so that a credit card's thickness of mouthpiece is showing above the tip of the reed (C).

4. Place the ligature (D) with the two screws in the back over the reed and mouthpiece to the level of the marking on the mouthpiece. Keep the two screws (E) on the lower portion of the reed.

5. Tighten the two screws.

Tuning

Before attempting to tune the saxophone, play it for a minute or two to warm it up. With written "C" (sounding E♭) as your tuning note, raise or lower the pitch by using a twisting motion to move the mouthpiece slightly in or out of the neck. Moving it in will raise the pitch and moving it out will lower the pitch (Fig. 5.5).

Mechanically speaking, this is about all you can do to tune a saxophone. However, there is more to playing any instrument in tune than just making a structural adjustment.

Figure 5.3.   Saxophone mouthpiece.

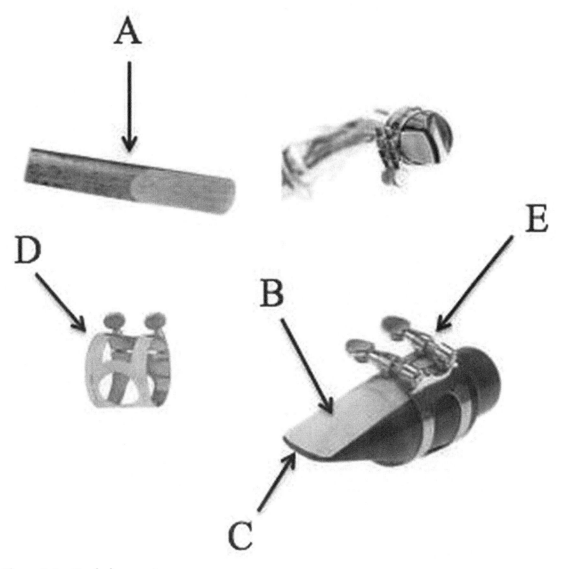

Figure 5.4. Reed placement.

All wind instruments depend on the player to produce the sound through his embouchure on a mouthpiece. The degree to which the player learns to control these two factors ultimately has the most profound effect on intonation.

The selection of the reed and the mouthpiece are the primary issues when striving for good intonation. These should be chosen with care and, if possible, with the guidance of a saxophone professional. (See the In-Depth section to follow on mouthpiece selection.) After the selection is made, playing in tune then becomes a matter of embouchure. Tighter or looser embouchures with proper placement of the mouthpiece in the mouth are the factors that then control pitch. It is subsequently up to the player to correct intonation.

Figure 5.5.   Twisting mouthpiece.

Sound Production: The Mouthpiece

The saxophone mouthpiece (Fig. 5.6) uses a single cane reed (A), which is attached to the mouthpiece (B) by a ligature (C). Figure 5.7 shows the parts of the saxophone mouthpiece. The facing on a mouthpiece, the flat side where the reed is placed, is one of the most important parts of any reed instrument for it is the facing in conjunction with the reed and the juxtaposition of the two that ultimately produce the sound.

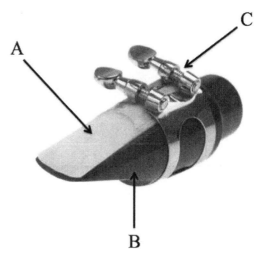

Figure 5.6.   Mouthpiece/reed/ligature.

Saxophone Mouthpiece

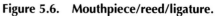

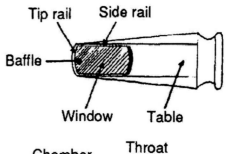

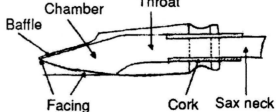

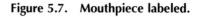

Figure 5.7.   Mouthpiece labeled.

Facing can be short, medium, or long. Following the basic concept that is true of musical instrument design—the bigger the instrument the lower the sound—longer facings favor lower sounds, shorter facings favor higher sounds, and medium facings strike a balance. The obvious conclusion is that a medium facing will probably be best for most students.

The Embouchure

The word *embouchure* refers to the position of the lips and facial muscles in relation to the mouthpiece when playing a wind instrument.

Each player's embouchure is unique since it is the product of the size, shape, and general structure of his oral facade. Below are some general rules and guidelines that can be followed when developing an embouchure. However, in order to be effective in achieving the best results in producing sound on a wind instrument, the embouchure will have to be developed by each individual under the supervision of a trained professional, the final product being unique to the individual. To set the embouchure:

1. Pull back the lower lip over the lower teeth just enough to form a pad for the teeth. Too much padding will restrict the reed vibration. Figure 5.7 shows a side view of a mouthpiece facing that gradually slopes away from the plane of the table. It is in this area that the reed is able to vibrate and produce a sound. Another way to see this space is to view the mouthpiece (with a reed in place) from the side with a light behind it. Note the point at which the reed leaves the plane of the mouthpiece. The reed vibrates from that point up.

2. Place the mouthpiece in the mouth with the reed resting on the lower lip at the exact point where the reed begins to slope away from the lay of the mouthpiece. That point will vary depending on the lip size and shape in conjunction with the lower teeth configuration. A bit of trial and error will help find the sweet spot that will produce a saxophone tone.

3. With the upper teeth placed firmly on top of the mouthpiece, close the lips around the mouthpiece with a slight smile, keeping the corners of the mouth firm so that no air can escape.

4. Keep the chin muscles firm and pulled down.

5. After all of the above, blow gently into the instrument adjusting it slightly in and out of the mouth until a proper saxophone sound occurs. When it does, the embouchure and playing position have been established.

6. When blowing into the instrument, keep the cheek muscles firm to avoid puffy cheeks.

Fingering

The saxophone key system consists of a basic set of six tone holes on the front of the body of the instrument (Fig. 5.8) and, depending on the design, an additional sixteen to eighteen tone holes placed in appropriate locations to complete the notes on the instrument. All the tone holes are covered by padded keys (Fig. 5.9).

The six basic tone holes are fingered by the index, middle, and third fingers of each hand. The left hand manipulates the upper three holes and the right hand manipulates the lower (Fig. 5.10). All the other keys are

Figure 5.8.   Basic tone holes.

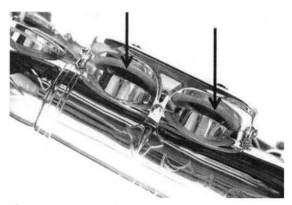

Figure 5.9.   Open key.

the fingering for a saxophone without a fingering chart, start with the first key depressed and then cover the open keys one at a time in descending order from the top down. Pressing the side keys will alter the tone produced when any or all of the six open holes are covered.

Figure 5.10.   Finger placement.

articulated by the thumb and pinky finger on each hand and the side of the index fingers.

When playing the saxophone, the effective length of the instrument is as long as the distance between the mouthpiece and the first open hole (Fig. 5.11A). As the holes are covered, the instrument becomes longer and the sound lower (Fig. 5.11B). To determine

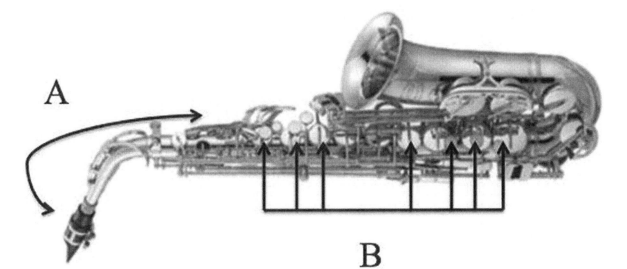

Figure 5.11. Effective length.

There are many fingerings that are very similar, if not the same, for the saxophone, oboe, and flute. Studying the charts for those instruments side by side will show patterns that will be helpful in determining fingering without having to resort to a fingering chart.

The diagram in Figure 5.12 shows the keys of a saxophone and how they are represented in the saxophone fingering chart.

Basic Saxophone Fingering Chart

To finger a note, depress the filled-in keys or levers in the drawing above the note. The side keys are articulated by the side of each hand at the first knuckle (Fig. 5.13).

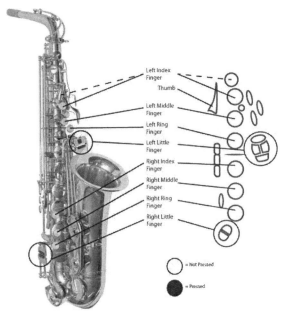

Figure 5.12. Fingering diagram.

Figure 5.13.   Fingering chart.

Expanded In-Depth Study

The Instrument

The saxophone is a quasi-inverted, S-shaped, conical brass tube beginning at the mouthpiece, at about the size of a dime, and ending up at the bell, where it is about the size of a teacup saucer (Fig. 5.14).

Figure 5.14. Saxophone.

Unlike most other musical instruments, the saxophone was conceived and invented by one individual, the Belgian clarinetist Adolphe Sax. It was his intention to bridge the gap between the brass and woodwind instrument sections of the orchestra by combining the features of both. The result was a brass instrument with holes in the body, which, when opened and closed, shorten or lengthen the effective sound-producing length of the instrument. The saxophone generates sound by a single-reed mechanism similar to that of the clarinet.

Due to the sax's unique—perhaps even radical—concept, there was and still continues to be a wide disparity of opinions regarding the virtues and shortcomings of the instrument. The saxophone has a range from B♭ below middle C to F♯ an octave above the treble staff. The instrument shortens or lengthens the vibrating column of air that produces sound through the use of from eighteen to twenty-one tone holes and two vent or octave keys.

The saxophone is a hybrid instrument that can produce such a variety of timbres that it can be used in jazz bands and symphony orchestras alike and can even accompany the human voice.

The Mouthpiece

The mouthpiece of the saxophone is often described as appearing to be very similar to that of the clarinet (Fig. 5.15). At first inspection of the two, this may seem reasonable. A closer evaluation, however, will show that whereas a clarinet mouthpiece is specifically designed to produce a distinct clarinet sound, when used by a professional, the saxophone mouthpiece

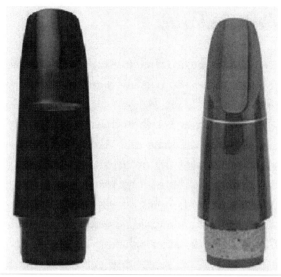

Figure 5.15.   Mouthpiece.

can produce a wide variety of sounds that satisfy the acoustical versatility of the instrument.

A vast number of changes have taken place in the design of the saxophone's mouthpiece since its inception in 1840. It has been lengthened, shortened, enlarged, made smaller, cored out, tapered, colored, and reshaped using every sort of material conceivable. Each of these changes has contributed to the wide variety of opinions of the sound of the instrument, since each change in mouthpiece design resulted in a change in tone quality or timbre.

In the preceding chapters, it was noted that the sound generators of the flute and clarinet (i.e., the head joint on the flute and the mouthpiece/reed on the clarinet) were almost entirely responsible for the quality and timbre of the instrument. This is also the case with the saxophone.

The design and names for the parts of the saxophone mouthpiece are like those of the clarinet. This explains why it is so easy to make an association with the two and to say simply that the saxophone uses a mouthpiece

that is similar to that of the clarinet. The differences, however, are found neither in the labels given to the parts nor in the general appearance of the two mouthpieces, but rather in the detail of the specifications of construction.

The parts of the saxophone mouthpiece, as seen in Figure 5.4, are named with much the same terminology as that of the clarinet. The parts are the bore, window of the throat, tone chamber, table, lay or facing, and baffle.

The materials from which the mouthpieces are made are also similar to those of the clarinet, namely, wood, glass or crystal, plastic, and rubber along with some use of metal such as gold and silver.

Because the saxophone produces tones that include overtones up to the sixteenth partial, greater in number than any other instrument, the mouthpiece must act not only as a medium to supply sound, but also as a device to control the abundance of sound resulting from the design of the instrument.

The early alto saxophone mouthpiece was constructed with a cylindrical bore and with no taper. The throat was round and the tone chamber was not consistent in size but instead had a bulbous portion preceding the window. The wall surfaces were concave, giving it a tone that was mellow and lacked the erasable edge often associated with the saxophone.

The 1930s saw the evolution of the era of the large dance band, which brought a demand for a sound that would be more compatible with brass instruments. At that time the reeds and brasses were distributed equally in these bands, and it became necessary to strengthen the sound of the reeds to match that of the brasses. Since the sophisticated devices for sound evaluation were not yet available, it was necessary for those involved in research and development to rely on instinct to find remedies. They experimented with materials of various densities and expansion coefficients and redesigned the structure of the mouthpiece interior. This experimentation produced a number of mouthpieces so unsatisfactory that they led to the decline of the reputation of the saxophone as a serious instrument.

During that time one mouthpiece—a modification of the original—was developed, which helped the saxophone regain some of its original popularity. It produced a richer tone with stronger emphasis on the upper partials. Subsequently, the industry developed an additional design modeled on the contours of the clarinet mouthpiece. This mouthpiece produced an extraordinarily powerful and penetrating sound, and it gained favor with those performers of dance band music who were in competition with their brass-playing counterparts. Simultaneously, the saxophone was removed from use by classical musicians, due to the instrument's increasing incompatibility with symphonic sounds.

Further experimentation with the aid of more advanced technological sound-evaluating devices led to smaller chambers, which proved to be unsatisfactory, and then to the double-tone chamber, which had a tapered cylindrical bore and a smaller tone chamber and throat. This mouthpiece produced a very aggressive sound, enabling a player literally to blast out the notes, but creating a greater likelihood that the less experienced player might lose control of tone quality and intonation.

A mouthpiece that seemed to strike a suitable balance, incorporating most of the attributes mentioned above, in proportions that produced a tone acceptable to most "classical" musicians, was designed in France. Featuring a round chamber, it produced a smooth, mellow tone yet included sufficient upper partials to still be bright.

Progress in the study of the technology of musical instruments increasingly shows that an instrument's source of sound holds the primary responsibility for the quality of that sound. To reiterate, the mouthpiece is the major contributing factor to the quality of the tone produced. For the saxophone, the mouthpiece has proven to be such an extreme example of this position that the player should select it with great care and consideration for her own aptitude, physical characteristics, embouchure, and playing experience.

The Body

The mouthpiece of the saxophone is coupled to the body through an L-shaped neck (Fig. 5.16A). The neck provides a convenient angle for placement of the mouthpiece in relation to the player's embouchure, and an appropriate placement for the primary octave or vent key (Fig. 5.16B).

The main body of the instrument is made of brass, is conical in shape, and uses a series of side holes that increase in size as they descend down the main structure. The body ends in an upturned bell with tone holes incorporated almost to the very end of the structure (Fig. 5.17).

The Key System

The key system of the saxophone uses principles that are similar to those of other woodwind instruments. One difference is that the pads on the keys of the saxophone are usually covered with leather instead of with fish skin or sheepskin (Fig. 5.18).

Figure 5.16.   Neck.

Figure 5.17.   Body.

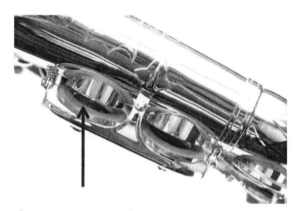

Figure 5.18.   Key pad.

This covering is necessary because the large size of the tone holes and the force of the strike of the key against the tone holes result in increased wear on the pads. The large size also causes the pads to be more susceptible to the accumulation of moisture from the player's breath and makes them subject to more rapid deterioration. Leather pads are stronger and hold up better under these conditions.

The pads cover a series of from eighteen to twenty-one tone holes depending on the model of the instrument. They are graduated in size, starting from the top where the smallest holes are located, to the largest holes at the lowest end of the body. The two vent or octave holes mentioned previously are located nearest the mouthpiece.

In order to produce the upper octave, it is necessary to divide the vibrating air column in the body of the instrument at the midpoint. This division is achieved through the use of two octave vents strategically placed to allow for acceptable but not perfect intonation on all notes (Fig. 5.19A and 5.19B).

Technically, in order to create a saxophone that plays every note in tune, it would be necessary to have an octave vent for each note. The complexity of such a mechanism would make it impractical, and so only two vents are used.

When the saxophone is at rest, some of the tone holes in the body are closed and others are open. An open key refers to a key that, when at rest, is not covering the hole it services (Fig. 5.20). In effect, that hole is open, but it has a key to cover it when necessary. A closed key refers to a key that, when at rest, covers and seals the hole it services (Fig. 5.21).

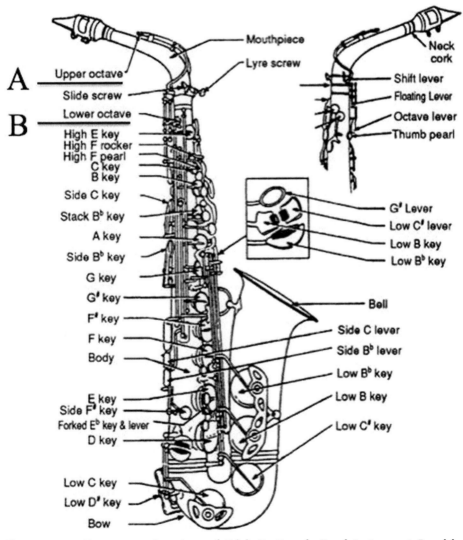

Figure 5.19. Key system (courtesy of Erick D. Brand, *Band Instrument Repairing Manual*).

Figure 5.20.   Open key.

Figure 5.21.   Closed key.

The Saxophone Family

The saxophone family has ten variations of the same instrument. Five currently in use are the soprano in B♭ (Fig. 5.22A), alto in E♭ (Fig. 5.22B), tenor in B♭ (Fig. 5.22C), baritone in E♭ (Fig. 5.22D), and the bass in B♭ (Fig. 5.22E).

The other five variations less commonly used are the sopranini in F and E♭, soprano in C, mezzo-soprano in F, melody in C, and the contrabass in E♭. While all ten instruments belong to the saxophone family, the second five are not readily available, and are not commonly found in the scores of much of today's music.

All of the saxophone models mentioned above are almost identical in fingering and playing requirements with only some adjustment needed to accommodate for the different size of the instrument and mouthpiece. These changes are minor and can easily be adapted by the player.

Key systems and fingering are the same, and all instruments are written in the treble clef in spite of the soprano, alto, tenor, baritone, and bass classifications. Notation is, therefore, identical, and the player can easily switch from one instrument to another without any concern for clef changes.

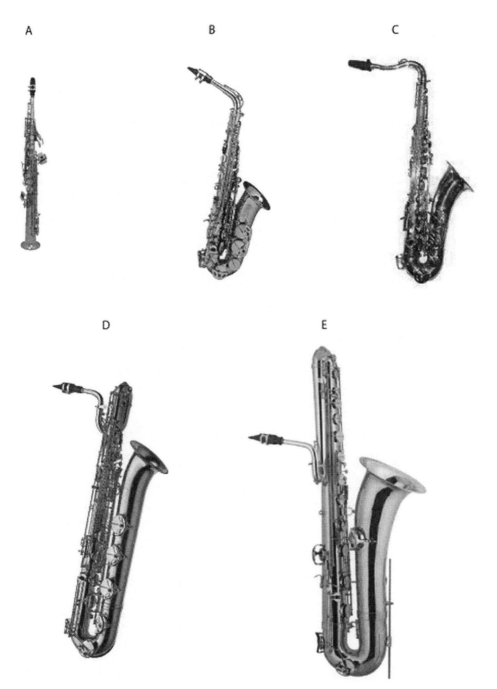

Figure 5.22. Saxophone family: A, B, C, D, E.

Summary

The saxophone holds a unique position in the woodwind family for a number of reasons. It is not made of wood but usually of brass (although there have been some made of silver and others of plastic); it is the only single-reed, conical instrument; it overblows at the octave; its tone quality can be radically changed by changing the mouthpiece; its intonation has so wide a range that the experienced player can capitalize on varying the pitch for special effects, though the amateur might have difficulty controlling pitch; and it can find a place in symphony, opera, and jazz either as part of an ensemble or as a solo instrument, all with equal prominence. It has come to be very widely known, and both loved and hated. The saxophone might be considered the only instrument capable of being all things to all people.

Chapter 6
The Oboe

Easy-Reference Quick Start

The Instrument

The oboe is built in three sections (Fig. 6.1): the upper joint (A), lower joint (B), and bell (C). This design evolved as a practical matter to allow for convenient packing and, in the event of damage, to facilitate the replacement of a part instead of the entire body of the instrument. A double reed is used in place of a mouthpiece (Fig. 6.2).

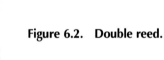

Figure 6.2.   Double reed.

Figure 6.1.   Oboe.

Assembly

1. Lubricate all the cork tenons with cork grease.
2. Hold the upper joint in your left hand and the lower joint in your right hand with your thumb on the first key (Fig. 6.3).
3. Work the upper joint gently into the lower using a twisting action, being sure to align the bridge key properly.
4. Using your left hand, depress the bell key with your thumb. Work the bell onto the lower joint using a twisting action (Fig. 6.4).
5. Insert the reed as far as it will go.

Playing Position

The general rule suggests holding the instrument at a forty-five-degree angle from the body. While playing a sustained note from

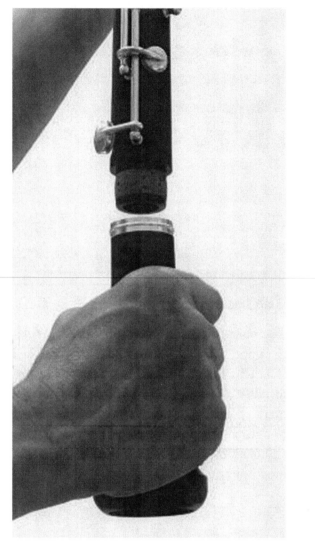

Figure 6.4.   Oboe bell assembly.

this position as a starting point, the player should move the instrument slightly closer and then farther from the body until the optimum angle for producing the best sound is found for that particular player.

Sound Production

The oboe uses a double reed (Fig. 6.5A) in place of a mouthpiece. A double reed is made up of two cane reeds bound together onto a metal tube called a staple (Fig. 6.5B). The staple is covered with cork (Fig. 6.5C) and joins the reed to the body of the instrument.

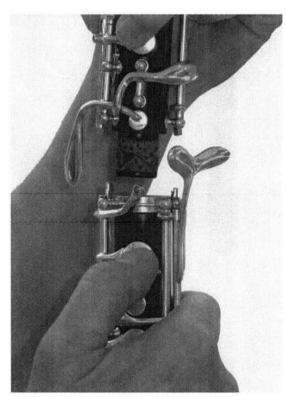

Figure 6.3.   Oboe joint assembly.

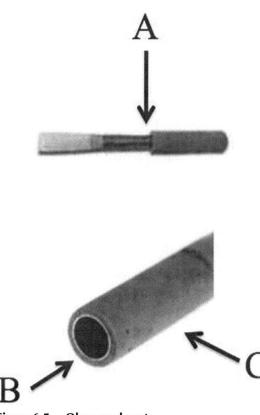

A

B

C

Figure 6.5. Oboe reed parts.

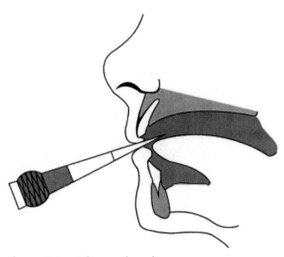

Figure 6.6. Oboe embouchure.

An oval-shaped opening is formed by the two blades of the reed, which vibrate against each other producing a sound. Before inserting the reed in the oboe, wet the reed by dipping it in water for approximately two minutes. Insert the reed into the top of the oboe as far as it will go.

Embouchure

The oboe requires a double embouchure. This is formed by folding the upper lip over the upper teeth and the lower lip over the lower teeth (Fig. 6.6). The corners of the mouth should be drawn inward. Do not puff the cheeks. When the reed is placed between the player's lips and air is blown into the ()-shaped opening that is formed by the two blades of the reed, the blades vibrate against each other to produce a sound.

The Single-Reed Alternative

A single-reed mouthpiece resembling a small version of a clarinet mouthpiece (Fig. 6.7) is available to enable a clarinet player to double on the oboe in a pinch. The single-reed oboe mouthpiece is also very convenient for younger students who may not be musically or physically mature enough to deal with all of the challenges of using a double reed. The user should bear in mind that the single-reed oboe mouthpiece is not a permanent substitute for the original sound generator, the double reed.

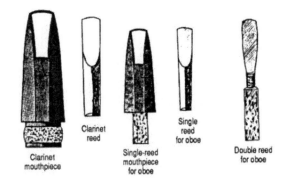

Clarinet mouthpiece

Clarinet reed

Single-reed mouthpiece for oboe

Single reed for oboe

Double reed for oboe

Figure 6.7. Reed mouthpieces.

Tuning

Since the double reed is the mouthpiece on an oboe, you might assume that tuning would be a simple matter of sliding the reed in to raise the pitch and out to lower the pitch. However, when you pull out the reed to lower the pitch, a space occurs between the bottom of the reed, the staple, and the bore of the instrument. This space interrupts the integrity of the reed/bore relationship, creating turbulence in the sound-producing vibrating column of air; this turbulence affects the tone quality and pitch. Those who ascribe to that theory prefer adjusting intonation via the embouchure/reed relationship. Adjusting your embouchure pressure and muscle position can alter the pitch up or down.

The note of choice to tune the oboe is usually "A" 440 (cycles per second). When played on the oboe, the note is traditionally used as the tuning guide for an orchestra. There is no scientific reason for this except to say that the oboe sound is clear, penetrating, and easy to hear above the cacophony of an orchestra tuning.

Fingering

The oboe is constructed with a basic set of six tone holes on the front of the body of the instrument. These are covered by keys and are fingered by the index, middle, and third finger of each hand (Fig. 6.8).

Additional tone holes are placed in appropriate locations on the body to complete the notes on the instrument. These holes are articulated by the thumb, pinky finger, and the side of the index fingers between the first and second knuckle on each hand (Fig. 6.9).

When playing the oboe, the effective length of the instrument is as long as the distance between the reed and the first open hole (Fig. 6.10). As the holes are covered, the instrument becomes longer and the sound lower.

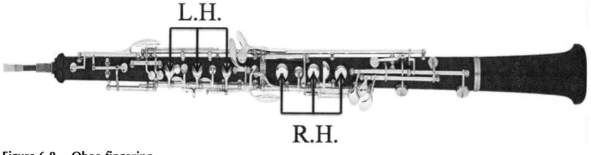

Figure 6.8. Oboe fingering.

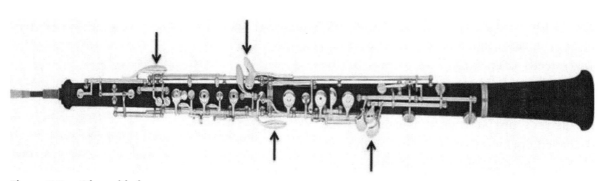

Figure 6.9. Oboe side keys.

Figure 6.10. Effective length.

Fingering for the oboe is more complex than for other woodwind instruments and, as such, is more difficult to figure out without referring to a chart. However, there are many oboe fingerings that are very similar, if not the same, as those of the saxophone and the flute. Studying the charts for those instruments side by side will show patterns that will be helpful in determining fingering without having to resort to a fingering chart.

The Key System

Figure 6.11 shows the key system of a full conservatory system oboe. Figure 6.12 shows a diagram of oboe keys and the fingers to be used for each key.

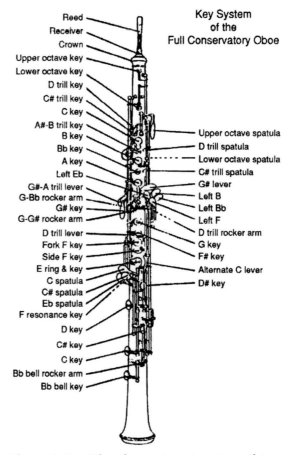

Figure 6.11. Oboe key system (courtesy of Lars Kirmser, *Woodwind Quarterly*).

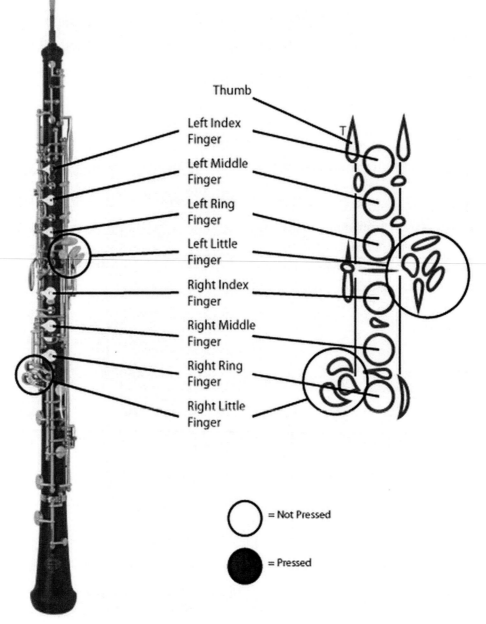

Figure 6.12.   Oboe fingering diagram.

Basic Oboe and English Horn Fingering Chart

To finger a particular note, depress the filled-in keys or levers below the note shown in the diagram. Low B and B♭ are not found on the English horn (Fig. 6.13).

The Oboe Family

The instruments that are considered to be in the oboe family are somewhat esoteric. These are seldom seen in use except when the score calls for them. They are the oboe d'amore in A, cor anglais or English horn in

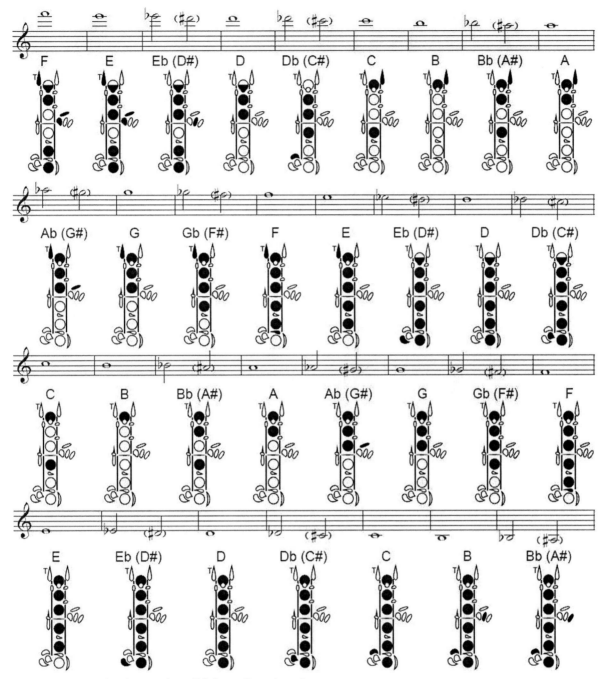

Figure 6.13. Basic oboe and English horn fingering chart.

**Examples
of the
Oboe Family**

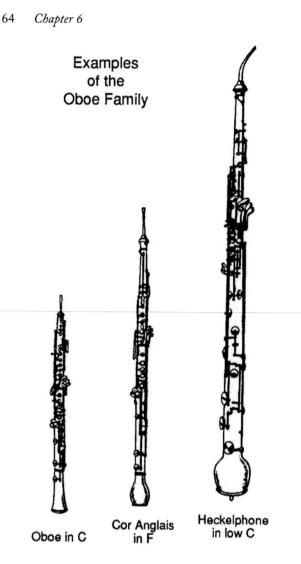

Oboe in C

Cor Anglais
in F

Heckelphone
in low C

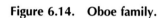

Figure 6.14.   Oboe family.

F, bass oboe in low C, and the heckelphone in low C. The cor anglais and heckelphone are depicted in Figure 6.14 for comparison with the oboe in C. All of these instruments transpose below the oboe in C by the interval of the key named.

Expanded In-Depth Study

Some information in this section is repeated for the convenience of the reader.

The Instrument

The body of the oboe is conical in shape and usually constructed of hardwood or plastic. It is designed with tone holes that are covered with a key mechanism consisting of levers, cups, and pads similar to but more complicated than that of the clarinet.

The cone-shaped bore of the oboe starts at the point of entry of the reed and is small in comparison with other woodwind instrument bores. Being conical, the oboe overblows at the octave. Because the cone is so small, it produces a tone that is rich in upper partials in relation to the fundamental. In fact, the instrument is capable of producing as many as twelve or more upper partials. These partials are extremely intense and, in some cases, are even capable of overpowering the fundamental. This is not to say that the fundamental is not audible to the listener, for the human ear, in conjunction with the central nervous system, is able to distinguish the intended pitch in spite of the ratio of the fundamental to its partners in sound.

The oboe's small conical bore and proportionately small side holes, in conjunction with the forceful nature of a double-reed sound generator, produce an intense spectrum of overtones above a fundamental. The resulting sound is reedy and concentrated, which is the sound that is distinctive and particular to the oboe.

The oboe has the longest list of ancestors of all the woodwinds. Although it resembles the clarinet in appearance, the oboe is in many ways more closely related to the flute and to the saxophone. It is like the flute in their similarity of fingering and in that they both overblow at the octave. It is similar to the saxophone in that they both have a conical bore and share similar fingerings.

The oboe is a derivative of the shawm, the most ancient woodwind instrument, and, as in the shawm, the sound on the oboe is generated by a double reed, which excites a column of air contained within a conical-shaped body. The instrument can be made of a variety of hardwoods, plastic, or, in rare instances, metal.

Sound Production: The Reed

The oboe has no mouthpiece. Its sound generator takes the form of a double reed (i.e., two cane reeds bound together onto a metal tube called a staple). The staple is covered with cork and joins the reed to the body of the instrument. When the reed is placed between the player's lips, and air is blown into the oval-shaped opening that is formed by the two blades of the reed, the blades vibrate against each other, activating the air column already present in the body of the instrument. The sound produced is then modified by the body and keys of the instrument. Also available is a single-reed mouthpiece, resembling a small version of the clarinet's mouthpiece. This mouthpiece will be discussed later in this chapter.

The oboe reed is simple in design. It is, however, the subject of much dismay, frustration, conflict, and despair among oboists. The sound generators of other instruments may be easily obtained, but oboists cannot go to the local music dealer and select a mouthpiece from an assortment of designs, materials, sizes, and shapes. Oboists are relegated to either making their own reeds that will, incidentally, have a relatively short life, or to depend on a reed maker for a steady supply. This dependence is unique to oboe players and to other players of double-reed instruments.

Although single-reed users also suffer anguishes related to reed usage, their plight is less serious than that of the double-reed user, as it is the mouthpiece of the single-reed instrument and not the reed alone that plays the most significant role as the true sound generator.

The double reed, which is constructed of cane, is by its very nature inconsistent. Each reed is unique in its structure. Even the same instrument played by the same performer can never reproduce exactly the same tone quality when a different reed is used.

The Single-Reed Oboe Mouthpiece

As stated above, one attempt at circumventing the inconsistency of the double reed was the

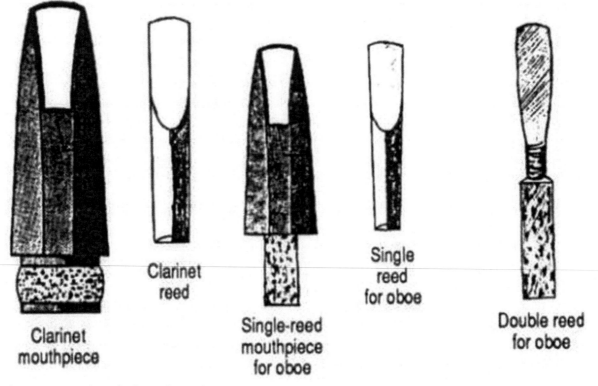

Figure 6.15.   Oboe single-reed mouthpiece.

introduction of the single-reed mouthpiece designed for use on a double-reed instrument (Fig. 6.15).

This mouthpiece copies the general structure and design of a clarinet mouthpiece but is adapted to the size and needs of an oboe or bassoon. The purpose of the device is to enable a clarinet player to double on the oboe in a pinch. When the music requires a short passage for an oboe, and the budget does not allow an oboist to be hired for this performance, the single-reed mouthpiece can be used. The single-reed oboe (or bassoon) mouthpiece is also very convenient for younger students who may not be musically or physically mature enough to deal with all of the challenges of using a double reed.

The use of the single-reed mouthpiece on the oboe has stirred up much controversy. It is this writer's opinion that there is a place for the mouthpiece in the overall scheme of music study and that, given certain circumstances, such a device can prove to be useful and can possibly even "save the day." Pragmatic but sparing use of any device that will extend the performance of music to those who need such aids is certainly advisable. But the user must also bear in mind that the single-reed oboe mouthpiece is not a permanent substitute for the original sound generator, the double reed.

An in-depth look at oboe reeds requires complex and lengthy research, and leads to inconclusive results. Research by experts who specialize in the area of oboe sound production indicate that there are still no definitive recommendations regarding what will produce the best sound on a double-reed instrument. There are still no final answers.

The Key System

During the past century and a half, a number of different key systems were tried in attempts to maximize the potential of the basic conical double-reed instrument. These were simple systems such as a thumb plate system, non-automatic octave keys, low B–C connections, an articulated E♭, a forked-F vent, an articulated G♯ thumb plate action, a half-hole plate, a semiautomatic octave key, and a fully automatic octave key. Other devices were added to and subtracted from the key system of the oboe in France, Germany, England, Spain, and other countries. The many key systems that were developed enjoyed varying degrees of success and longevity.

All of these separate systems evolved into what is now referred to as the conservatory system (Fig. 6.16) developed by Lucien Lorée and Georges Gillet between 1900 and 1906. Today it is generally referred to as the plateau or French system. But, in fact, the saga does not end there, for there are a number of variations of this system. These are the basic conservatory, modified conservatory, standard conservatory, and full conservatory models. They are all modifications of the original design of Lorée and Gillet. Figure 6.17 shows a chart of the different systems.

A point of interest to the music educator/technician is that in spite of the preference for plateau keys by professional performers, the ring type key (similar to that found on the clarinet) is recommended for school use. The ring system is less likely to go out of adjustment and is found to be more suited to the physical stress to which a school instrument may be subjected.

The oboe key system has an insatiable desire to be adjusted. Due to the complexity of the system and the variety of possible accessory keys, the instrument can have as many as seventeen adjustment screws. Each of these screws regulates two or more keys so that their reciprocal function will be operational. It is recommended that adjustments be made judiciously and only by a professional technician, if possible.

Figure 6.18 is a diagram of the adjustment system for a full conservatory oboe. This

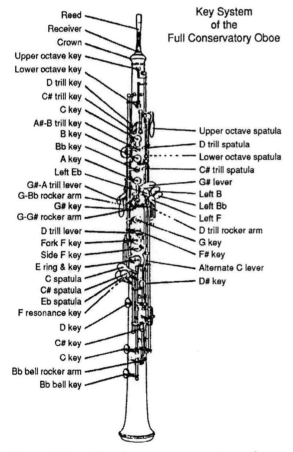

Figure 6.16. Oboe key system (courtesy of Lars Kirmser, *Woodwind Quarterly*).

Reed
Receiver
Crown
Upper octave key
Lower octave key
D trill key
C# trill key
C key
A#-B trill key
B key
Bb key
A key
Left Eb
G#-A trill lever
G-Bb rocker arm
G# key
G-G# rocker arm
D trill lever
Fork F key
Side F key
E ring & key
C spatula
C# spatula
Eb spatula
F resonance key
D key
C# key
C key
Bb bell rocker arm
Bb bell key

Key System of the Full Conservatory Oboe

Upper octave spatula
D trill spatula
Lower octave spatula
C# trill spatula
G# lever
Left B
Left Bb
Left F
D trill rocker arm
G key
F# key
Alternate C lever
D# key

System	No. of Keys	Plateau	Range	Trill	Bell	Other
Basic Conservatory	15	6	low B	F#-G# D♭-E♭ Hi C-D Hi B-C	no	
Modified Conservatory	16	6	low B♭	same + A♭-B♭	yes	forked F resonance key
Standard Conservatory	18	6	low B♭	same + G#-A C-C# D#-E	yes	same
Full Conservatory	19	6	low B♭	same + low B-C#	yes	left hand F

Figure 6.17. Additional oboe key systems.

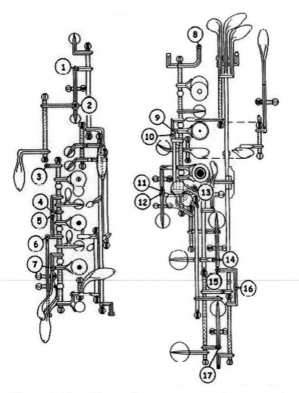

Figure 6.18. Oboe adjustment screws (courtesy of Lars Kirmser, *Woodwind Quarterly*).

diagram is offered not as a guide to adjusting but rather as a visual example of the complexity of the system in an effort to discourage any attempt by a novice to make an adjustment.

The Oboe Family

In addition to the oboe in C, there are four other similar instruments often referred to as deep oboes. These are the oboe d'amore in A, the cor anglais or English horn in F, the bass oboe in low C, and the heckelphone in low C.

The cor anglais and heckelphone are depicted in Figure 6.19 for comparison with the oboe in C. All of these instruments transpose below the oboe in C by the interval of the key named. They share almost all of the characteristics of the oboe in C, using a double reed on a conical body controlled by a complex key system over a side-hole system.

In addition to their varying ranges, significant differences are in the transpositions and the addition of a metal crook at the top and a bulbous bell at the bottom.

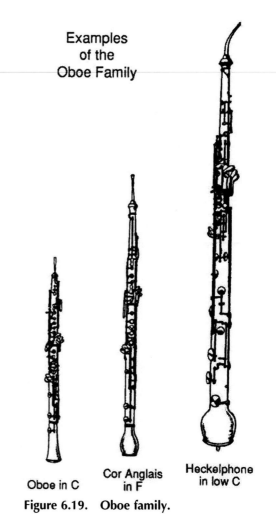

Examples
of the
Oboe Family

Oboe in C

Cor Anglais
in F

Heckelphone
in low C

Figure 6.19. Oboe family.

Summary

The oboe comes from one of the oldest methods of wind instrument music-making. It evolved from the primitive act of squeezing together the ends of a cut reed, and blowing air through the small space remaining to excite a vibration. It developed into a highly complicated woodwind instrument, producing sounds of great intensity; it is regarded by many as one of the most sophisticated of the modern orchestral instruments. It is challenging to learn, difficult to play, expensive to purchase, and demanding in its maintenance requirements, but still the tonal jewel of the ensemble.

Chapter 7

The Bassoon

Easy-Reference Quick Start

The Instrument

The bassoon is constructed of five sections, which are connected by cork-covered tenons similar to those used on the clarinet and oboe (Fig. 7.1). The first and smallest section of the bassoon is the bocal, or crook, which is made of metal (A). It serves as the receiver for the reed. Traveling from the bocal down in a U shape are the wing or tenor joint (B), boot or double joint (C), bass or long joint (D), and bell joint (E) for a total of about eight feet.

There are presently two different models or designs of bassoons in use. These are the French and the German. The difference is primarily in the key mechanism and will be explained in more detail under fingering in the In-Depth section to follow.

Assembly

1. Lubricate all tenons with cork grease.
2. Holding the bass joint in your left hand and the wing joint in your right hand, line up the two so the bottom tenons are even (Fig. 7.2).
3. Insert the two sections into the boot joint (Fig. 7.3).
4. Add the bell joint, being careful to align the bridge key (Fig. 7.4).
5. Add the bocal, being careful not to damage the key (whisper key) that covers the nipple on the bocal (Fig. 7.5).
6. Secure the body lock located on the lower part of the instrument to join the bass and wing joints (Fig. 7.6).

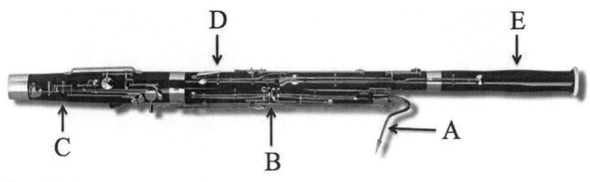

Figure 7.1. Bassoon.

Figure 7.3.   Assembling the bassoon boot.

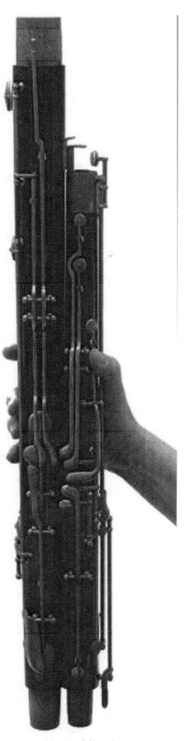

Figure 7.2.   Assembling bassoon joints.

Figure 7.4.   Assembling the bassoon bell.

Figure 7.5.   Assembling the bassoon crook.

Figure 7.6.   Bassoon lock.

7. Add the crutch or hand rest also located on the lower section of the instrument to support the right hand (Fig. 7.7).

Playing Position

Due to its weight, the bassoon requires a seat strap, neck strap, or shoulder harness for support. The choice is individual. Place the left

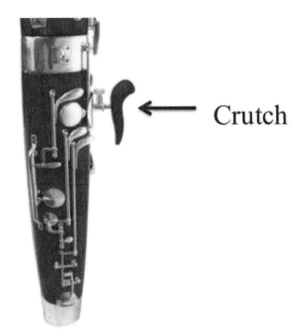

Figure 7.7.   Bassoon crutch.

hand in position to cover the three tone holes in front of the wing joint with your first, second, and third fingers (Fig. 7.8A).

Using the right hand on the bass joint, cover the two tone holes and the plateau key below them with the first, second, and third finger (Fig. 7.8B). All the other keys on the front of the instrument are fingered by the pinky finger of each hand.

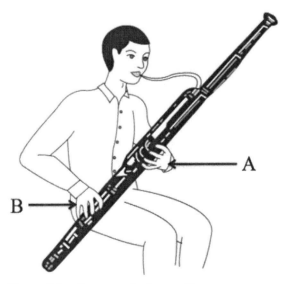

Figure 7.8.   Bassoon playing position.

The thumbs are used to finger the twelve keys on the back of the instrument. The number of keys on the back can vary with the model of instrument. A crutch (refer back to Figure 7.7) can be attached to the boot joint to support the right hand.

Sound Production

The bassoon uses a double reed in place of a mouthpiece (Fig. 7.9). A double reed is made up of two cane reeds bound together by three metal wires and a cord winding. An oval-shaped opening is formed by the two blades of the reed, which vibrate against each other producing a sound.

Figure 7.9.   Bassoon reed.

Before inserting the reed on the bocal, wet the reed by dipping it in water for approximately two to three minutes. Insert the reed into the bocal as far as it will go.

Embouchure

The embouchures used to play most wind instruments usually take a standardized form that is generally accepted. Most players end up agreeing on essentially the same or a very similar oral setting. Unfortunately, this is not the case for the bassoon.

Like the oboe, the bassoon requires a double embouchure, meaning that both the upper and lower lips are in direct contact with the reed. The bassoon double embouchure is somewhat more relaxed than that of the oboe and does not rely as much on the upper and lower teeth for support. The most commonly agreed upon recommendations for setting a bassoon embouchure are as follows:

1. Lower the jaw as if yawning.
2. Pucker the lips as if blowing air or whistling.
3. There are some disagreements about drawing the lips into the mouth to pad the teeth and provide a soft surface on which to rest the reed. Some recommend to do so but caution not to interfere with the vibration of the reed. Others suggest that only the lower teeth should be covered and the upper lip should be in direct contact with the reed with no teeth support. Still others recommend that the upper and lower lips should control the reed with little or no teeth support, the issue being that too much pressure will stifle the sound.
4. All agree that pulling in the corners of the mouth like closing a drawstring bag is essential to sealing the embouchure to prevent any air leakage.
5. Other opinions include setting the jaw in an overbite position, putting the reed three quarters into the mouth, or placing the reed in the mouth up to the first wire band.

A simple but perhaps most practical recommendation for a beginner is to:

1. Lower the jaw.
2. Draw the lower lip in a bit to receive some support from the lower teeth.

3. Place the reed on the lower lip and close the mouth firmly around the reed.
4. Draw the corners of the mouth inward.
5. Without puffing the cheeks, blow gently into the reed while moving it in or out until what is commonly referred to as the "crow" sound is produced.

This is a not-too-musical sound much like one produced by a crow in despair. At that position, the player has the start of what can develop into a most productive embouchure.

Figure 7.10 shows a diagram with both lips slightly drawn into the mouth, padding the teeth, and the reed partially inserted into the mouth. The amount of lip turned in and the amount of reed inserted between the lips must be adjusted to determine at what point the reed will vibrate in a controlled manner to produce the best sound.

The Single-Reed Bassoon Mouthpiece

A single-reed mouthpiece (Fig. 7.11), a small version of a clarinet mouthpiece, is available to enable a clarinet player to double on the

Figure 7.11. Bassoon single-reed mouthpiece.

bassoon in a pinch. The single-reed bassoon mouthpiece is also very convenient for younger students who are usually not musically or physically mature enough to deal with all of the challenges of using a double reed. The user should bear in mind that the single-reed bassoon mouthpiece is not a permanent substitute for the original sound generator, the double reed.

Tuning

The bassoon is a relatively inflexible instrument and, therefore, difficult to tune. The lower register is all but set by the manufacturer. Adjusting the bocal will have little effect on the general intonation. True tuning of a bassoon remains a product of the quality of the bocal, reed, the embouchure of the player, and his ability to finesse the pitch of the various notes.

Fingering

There are two different types of bassoon key systems currently in use, the German system and the French system. The German, or

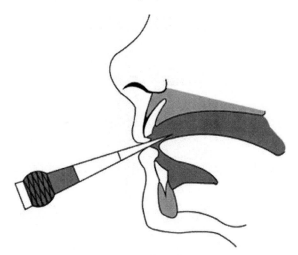

Figure 7.10. Bassoon embouchure.

Heckel, system bassoon contains from twenty-one to twenty-four keys, depending on the sophistication of the model. The French key system is mechanically simpler and relies more on the player's virtuosity to achieve the transitions from note to note.

A significant number of bassoonists in Europe use the French system. American bassoonists almost exclusively use the German system. Figure 7.12 is a diagram of the bassoon keys showing which fingers are used for each key.

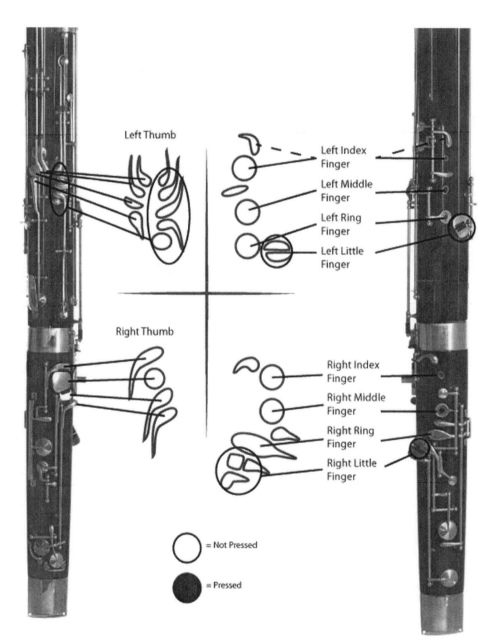

Figure 7.12.   Bassoon fingering diagram.

Basic Bassoon Fingering Chart

To finger a particular note, depress the keys or levers filled in or cover the holes filled in. Unfilled in indicates either a hole or key left untouched (Fig. 7.13).

The Bassoon Family

The only additional relative to the bassoon that is in use with some degree of regularity is the double bassoon, or contrabassoon, which sounds an octave lower than the bassoon (Fig. 7.14).

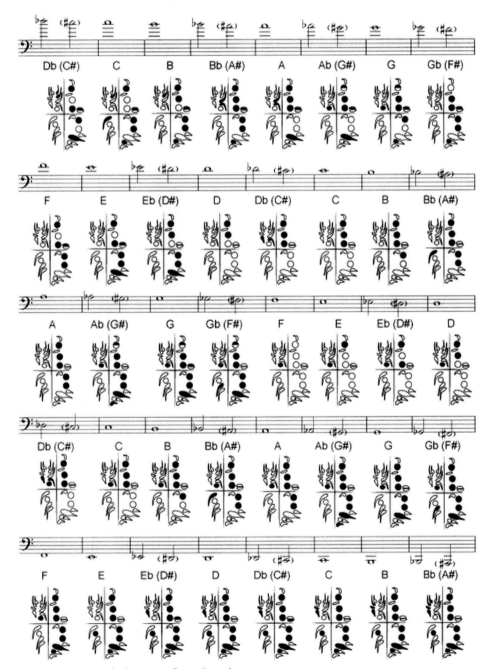

Figure 7.13. Basic bassoon fingering chart.

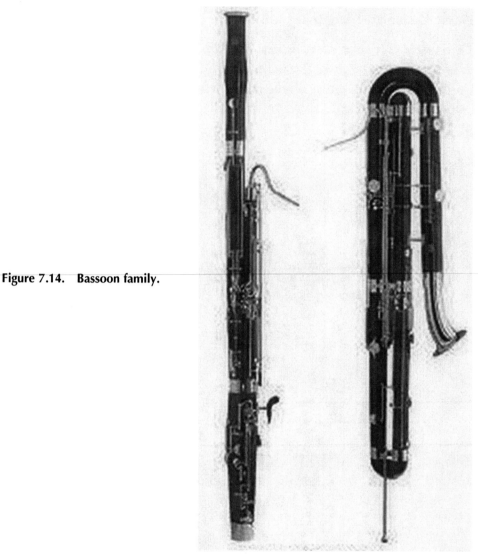

Figure 7.14.   Bassoon family.

Expanded In-Depth Section

The Instrument

The bassoon shares many of the historical, physical, and mechanical characteristics of the oboe. The body of the bassoon has a conical bore and uses a body tone-hole system served by a mechanical padded-key system like that of all other woodwind instruments.

Bassoons are considered by many to be acoustical enigmas and, as such, are the instru-ments most challenging to understand, build, and play.

The instrument has a conical bore, and is about eight feet (2.5 m) long. It is separated into five sections that are assembled using the tenon design (Fig. 7.15A), similar to that used in the clarinet and oboe. The smallest section of the bassoon is the bocal (Fig. 7.15B). Made of metal, it serves as the receiver for the reed

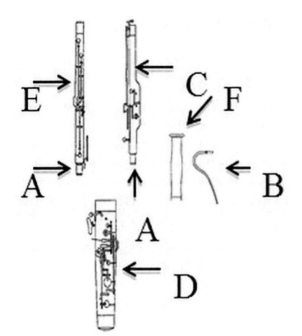

Figure 7.15. Bassoon parts.

An interesting aspect of the design of the bassoon is that the rate of expansion of the bore is half that of the oboe. Another design feature particular to the bassoon is that the tone holes at some points need to travel as far as two inches (five centimeters) to reach the bore. These must be drilled at an angle so that the bore end of the hole will be positioned to achieve the pitches desired and yet enable the player to span the distance with the fingers on the exterior of the body (Fig. 7.16).

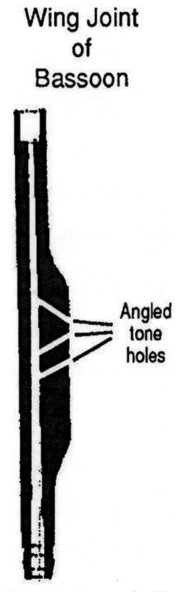

Figure 7.16. Bassoon wing joint.

and connects that sound generator (reed) to the body of the instrument.

The bore at the bocal is about one-eighth of an inch (three millimeters) in diameter. The bore progresses through the body, or amplifier, which consists of the wing joint (Fig. 7.15C), boot joint (Fig. 7.15D), bass joint (Fig. 7.15E), and bell joint (Fig. 7.15F). The bore ultimately reaches a final diameter of about 1.5 inches (3.8 centimeters) at the bell. These sections of the bassoon are usually made of maple, although other woods, ebonite, and occasionally metal are used. Because the bassoon is about eight feet long, it is folded in half at about the midpoint by the use of a U-bend called the boot (Fig. 7.15D).

Bassoons are now made in two types, the long-bore and short-bore models. The long-bore instrument produces a darker tone and is believed by many to produce truer intonation. The short-bore bassoon is more difficult to control and, therefore, is less consistent in its intonation.

This particular requirement results in a weakening of the venting (interrupting the vibrating column of air to reach upper registers), which allows a great portion of the energy to travel to the lower section of the instrument. The result is the strong resonance that is so particular to the sound of the bassoon.

Sound Production

The sound generator for the bassoon is the double reed. Like the oboe, the bassoon has no mouthpiece and so it shares all of the problems of sound production discussed in the previous chapter on the oboe, but with a few additions.

Bassoon reeds are consistently inconsistent. It can be expected that no two reeds will be alike. Therefore, there will be no two reeds producing exactly the same sound even though they are used by the same performer and on the same instrument. This inconsistency occurs because good bassoon reeds are most often individually made by hand and are the product of the skills or limitations of the maker. In addition, the raw material, cane, is by its very nature lacking in consistency, and is so delicate that the life span of a bassoon reed is relatively short. This combination of factors creates a potential for problems of sound production on the bassoon that require much dedicated attention and expertise.

Bassoon reeds are made in a variety of sizes, shapes, densities, and designs. There are usually ten parts to the design or shaping of the reed. If one were to multiply the number of variables by the number of parts where those variations might occur, the likelihood of arriving at a clinical description of a bassoon reed becomes almost impossible. It is possible to be aware of the design, structure, fabrication process, and assorted possible styles of

reeds commonly in use. This information can serve as a base from which to work in developing opinions and for gathering additional knowledge on the subject.

Figure 7.17 is a diagram of the parts of a bassoon reed showing its two major sections, the lay and the tube. The tube, consisting of the lower half, starts at the shoulder and contains the first wire (sometimes the references to first and second wire are reversed); the throat, or second wire; and the binding, under which there is a third wire. The upper half of the reed, called the lay, consists of the vibrating portion of the reed and includes the tip, which is the most sensitive portion of the reed.

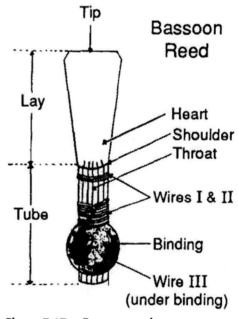

Figure 7.17.   Bassoon reed.

Bassoon reeds, like the instruments they serve, are classified as being either German or French in construction. The difference between them is primarily in the thickness of the lay, or heart, of the reed. German reeds tend to be thicker in the heart, whereas the French reed has a more gradual and even taper. This difference can be seen by holding the reed

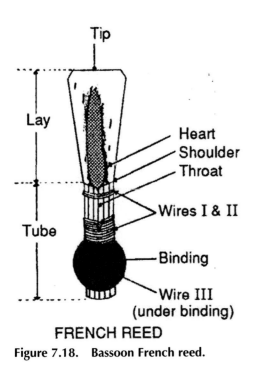

FRENCH REED

Figure 7.18. Bassoon French reed.

up to a strong light. The center of the lay is shadowed on the German reed, whereas on the French reed the light passes through more evenly (Fig. 7.18 and Fig. 7.19).

This difference can also be felt by gently passing the heart of the reed between the

thumb and index finger. The German reed will have a bulge down the center of the lay, while the French reed will feel flat. As a result of this structural difference, the French reed produces a thinner, more penetrating sound, while the German reed has a more haunting and darker sound.

The next characteristic that must be considered when examining a bassoon reed is the longitudinal contour of the lay. There are three possible contours that are used in double-reed manufacturing. These are the parallel contour, the wedge type, and the double-wedge contour (Fig. 7.20).

Bassoon Reeds

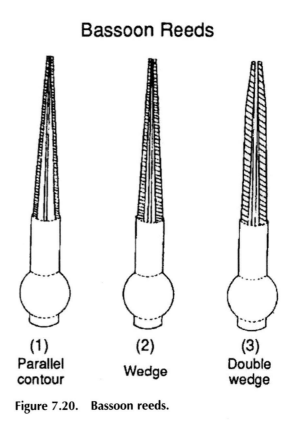

(1)
Parallel contour

(2)
Wedge

(3)
Double wedge

Figure 7.20. Bassoon reeds.

The parallel contour (1) is constructed so that both blades are of equal thickness throughout. This design is not commonly used because it is difficult to make and presents a problem to the player in maintaining control of pitch and tone quality.

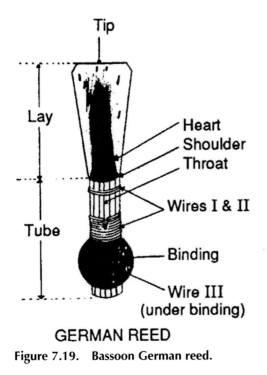

GERMAN REED

Figure 7.19. Bassoon German reed.

The wedge contour (2), where the blades gradually taper or thin out toward the tip, is used primarily in the construction of the French style reed. This design is more popular and easier to fabricate.

The double-wedge contour (3), used primarily for the German design reed, has many variations because it uses two degrees of taper. The first section of the blades shows a very slight taper or, sometimes, none at all. The second section of the blades then tapers more abruptly toward the tip of the reed. The length of the two sections of taper can vary significantly, according to the needs of the player and the design used by the reed maker.

The Key System

The key system for the bassoon is illustrated in Figure 7.21. The two different types of bassoons currently in use—the German system and the French system—are similar in appearance; however, there are considerable differences in the number of keys and how they are used.

The manner in which the keys function is, for the most part, the same as that of the other woodwind instruments. Padded cups cover holes, and the cups are interconnected and controlled by the player's depressing spatulas or finger plates. Posts, pivot screws, screw rods and tubes, wire springs, and flat springs are all present in some form, and all of these conform to the descriptions of the key systems in earlier chapters.

In spite of all the similarities of design, there remains one profound difference between the French and German key systems. The German system bassoon contains many more keys, especially in the boot joint. Specifically, the German system, sometimes referred to as the Heckel system—after the family of

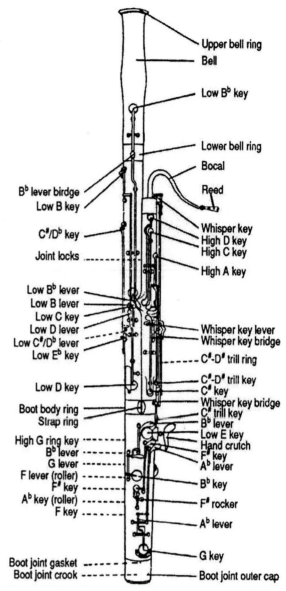

Figure 7.21. Bassoon key system (courtesy of Lars Kirmser, *Woodwind Quarterly*).

the same name that owns the world's most famous bassoon factory—will contain from twenty-one to twenty-four keys, depending on the sophistication of the model.

Additional features are assorted rollers to facilitate a smooth transition from one key to another, an automatic whisper key, assorted trill keys, ring keys, key guards, joint locks, an extended range, posts and springs that are locked in place with screws, metal-lined tone holes, extra octave keys, and half-hole keys such as those found on the oboe.

All of the extras on this rather lengthy list are "extra" only in the sense that a bassoon could be played without most of them. They are available on the Heckel, or German model bassoon, and facilitate the playing of the instrument and improve its intonation and life span. These parts are fabricated of nickel silver, German silver, or brass.

The French key system permits the player to perform the same music, but the system is mechanically simpler and relies more on the player's virtuosity to achieve the transitions from note to note. The French instruments also contain trill keys, finger plates and rings, rollers, and many of the other devices found in the German design. However, many notes are attainable only by using cross fingerings, half holing (rolling the finger off the hole to cover only half the hole), or trilling certain notes by means other than trill keys specifically designed to facilitate that particular trill.

Although the German system appears to be the system of choice, a significant number of bassoonists in Europe still use bassoons built on the French system; American bassoonists almost exclusively use the German system.

The Bassoon Family

The only additional relative to the bassoon that is in use with some degree of regularity is the double bassoon, or contrabassoon (Fig. 7.22), which sounds an octave lower than the bassoon. The instrument is designed not as an extension of the bassoon but as a different entity. There have been several other bassoons developed during the past century. Among them are the tenor, tenoroon, and soprano bassoons. These instruments are not commonly in use at this time.

Figure 7.22. Bassoon family.

Summary

The bassoon provides the lower notes of the woodwind choir. Considered by some to be the clown of instruments because of its ability to produce sounds that can evoke humor in the musical psyche, it is far from humorous in its design or the demands it places on its players. On the opposite side of the spectrum is its ability to transmit a solemnity, graphically demonstrated in the opening measures of Tchaikovsky's Sixth Symphony, the Pathétique.

In spite of the bassoon's large size, the successful work of its developers has made it possible for a skilled bassoonist to manipulate the instrument musically. There are many passages that are impressively rapid and complex, which can be performed confidently and competently by the professional bassoonist.

Technologically speaking, the instrument is consistent with its woodwind relatives in the maintenance demands of its sound generator, sound amplifier, and key work. The only possible exception might be that the keys are long and numerous and, therefore, may need more frequent regulation. Considering the acoustical and technological complexities created by the use of a double reed on a large, conical instrument, it appears that the bassoonist must function in an atmosphere of compromise if the instrument is to respond effectively.

The bassoon cannot operate for more than one octave without sacrificing quality, and so the reed, which cannot be changed in mid-passage, must be designed so that it will function reasonably effectively in all registers, at the expense of not being at its best in any one given register.

Does this mean that becoming involved with a bassoon as a technician is indeed to make a commitment to a life of challenge and frustration? Perhaps not! This may be one of the areas of musical instrument technology for an aspiring technician to make a mark in the industry by creating a redesigned bassoon that will produce the unique sound for which it is known without all of the negative characteristics inherent in the present instrument.

Chapter 8

Brass Instruments

Easy-Reference Quick Start

Principles of Fingering

The traditional introduction to fingering on any instrument begins with one note at a time as individual topics, which are accompanied by a chart illustrating all of the fingerings for that instrument.

Using this approach, it is easy to overlook the fact that almost every instrument has a simple, repetitious pattern that, when understood in its totality, significantly facilitates determining fingering for all notes of the instruments in that choir.

Understanding the System of Valves

Brass instruments are similar in their acoustical and structural designs. Sound is produced by the player's lips buzzing into a cup-shaped mouthpiece. A player can produce a series of open tones without the use of valves. Valves can then be used individually or in combination to lower open tones and produce other tones. When a valve is depressed, the holes

in the valve are realigned with an additional length of tubing that is part of the instrument. Longer tubing on an instrument produces lower pitches.

Figure 8.1 shows two types of valves. The piston valve is used on most brass instruments. The rotary valve is always used on the French horn and less frequently on other instruments.

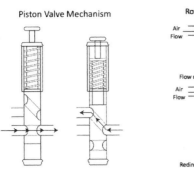

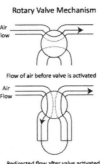

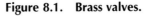

Figure 8.1.   Brass valves.

The Fingering Pattern

The trumpet will be used as an example for all valve instruments. Trumpets produce the following open tones with no valves depressed (Fig. 8.2). By depressing valves, the open tones can be lowered in half-step increments to produce the tones that exist between each open tone. So to lower an open tone one half step (a minor second), depress valve 2 (Fig. 8.3).

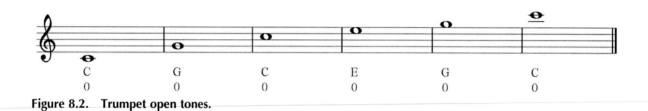

Figure 8.2.   Trumpet open tones.

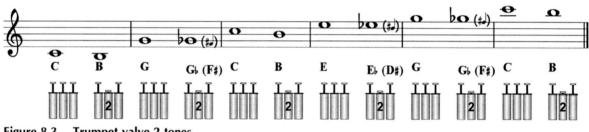

Figure 8.3.   Trumpet valve 2 tones.

To lower an open tone two half steps (a second), depress valve 1 (Fig. 8.4). To lower an open tone three half steps (a minor third), depress valve 3 or valves 1 and 2 (Fig. 8.5). Note: For better intonation the preferred fingering for these notes is 1 and 2.

To lower an open tone four half steps (a major third), depress valves 2 and 3 (Fig. 8.6). To lower an open tone five half steps (a perfect fourth), depress valves 1 and 3 (Fig. 8.7). To lower an open tone six half steps (augmented fourth or diminished fifth), depress valves 1, 2, and 3 (Fig. 8.8).

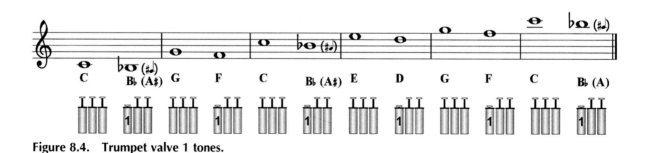

Figure 8.4.   Trumpet valve 1 tones.

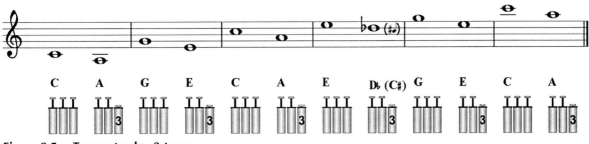

Figure 8.5.   Trumpet valve 3 tones.

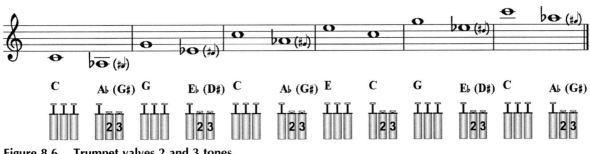

Figure 8.6.   Trumpet valves 2 and 3 tones.

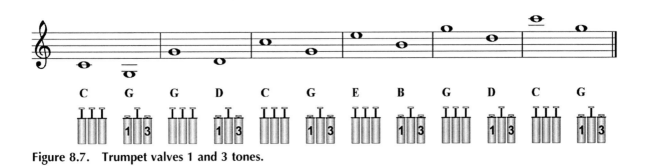

Figure 8.7.   Trumpet valves 1 and 3 tones.

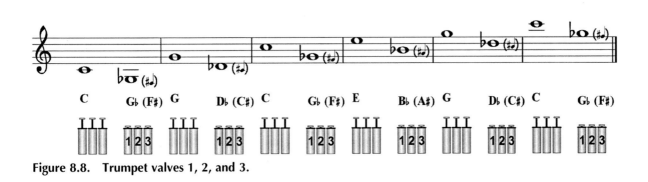

Figure 8.8.   Trumpet valves 1, 2, and 3.

Review

The valves on any brass instrument can be used individually or in combination, lowering an open tone to produce all the other tones that exist below the open tones. The pattern is as follows:

Valve 1 = whole step or a second
Valve 2 = half step or minor second
Valve 3 = step and a half or minor third
Valves 1 and 2 = step and a half or a minor third

Valves 2 and 3 = two whole steps or a major third
Valves 1 and 3 = two and a half steps or a perfect fourth
Valves 1, 2, and 3 = three whole steps or a diminished fourth

To determine the fingering without a fingering chart for any valve instrument, locate the open tones and apply the above principles.

Brass Sound Production

To produce a tone on a brass instrument, buzz moistened lips into a cup-shaped mouthpiece with the upper lip producing the primary buzz. Depending on the lip formation of the player, the lower lip generally buzzes to a lesser degree. The lower lip also provides support, acts as a stabilizer for the vibration of the lips, and controls the size of the opening through which the air passes into the mouthpiece.

Experts agree that placement of the mouthpiece on the lips is unique to each embouchure and must ultimately be determined by the player. To start, it is recommended that the mouthpiece be placed in the center of the lips with equal amounts of the upper and lower lip in contact with the mouthpiece cup. It is then a matter of adjusting the mouthpiece placement up or down until the position that produces the best sound for that individual is determined.

The pitches produced can be changed by increasing or decreasing the intensity of the buzz. This is accomplished by raising or lowering the corners of the mouth. Pulling the corners of the mouth down will raise the pitch, raising the corners of the mouth will lower the pitch.

Tuning All Brass Instruments

Because all brass instruments have inherent intonation problems, it is almost impossible to achieve tuning perfection.

Tuning a brass instrument is achieved by moving slides in or out. The main tuning slide is used to tune the instrument's basic pitch. Additional slides are used to tune the notes related to the use of each valve. Extending a slide will lower the pitch. Drawing a slide in will raise the pitch.

Certain brass instruments such as the euphonium and BB♭ tuba are structured with an auxiliary set of tubing that is used to compensate for the natural rise in pitch inherent in the low register of these instruments. By depressing a fourth valve, additional tubing is opened to lower the pitch for that particular note. This mechanism does not affect the other registers on the instrument.

Chapter 9

Brass Instruments

Fingering Charts

The major portion of the trumpet (Fig. 9.1) is cylindrical and contains valves that can be either of the piston or rotary type.

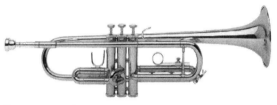

Figure 9.1. Trumpet.

Basic Trumpet and Cornet Fingering Charts

The cornet (Fig. 9.2) is similar to the trumpet in some respects; however, it is almost totally conical. The fingering is the same for both the trumpet (Fig. 9.3) and the cornet (Fig. 9.4).

Figure 9.2. Cornet.

Figure 9.3. Basic trumpet fingering chart.

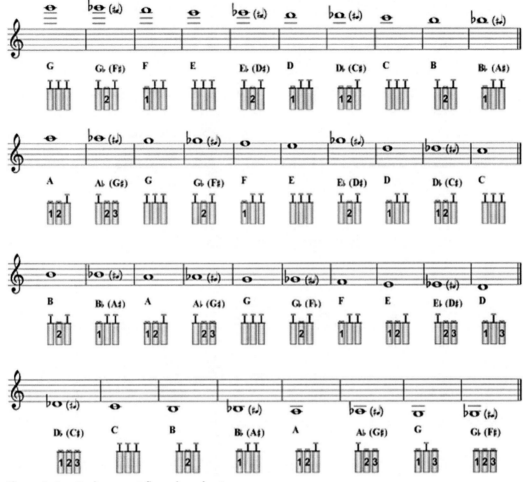

Figure 9.4.   Basic cornet fingering chart.

Basic Flugelhorn Fingering Chart

Figure 9.5.   Flugelhorn.

The flugelhorn (Fig. 9.5) is, in effect, a bass trumpet. It has the same range and pitch as the trumpet but demonstrates its unique characteristics in the contralto range, where it produces a tone that has a rich, mellow timbre. The fingering for the flugelhorn is the same as that of the trumpet (Fig. 9.6).

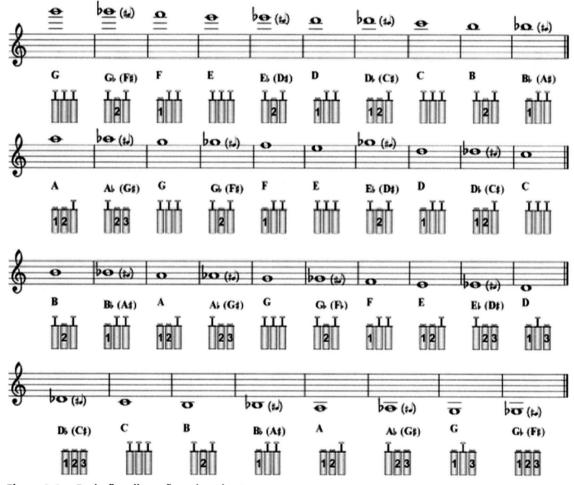

Figure 9.6.   Basic flugelhorn fingering chart.

The French Horns

The three French horns currently in use are the horns in F, B♭, and the double horn (F and B♭ combined). See Figure 9.7.

French horns use rotary valves, which function differently from piston valves but produce the same results of lowering fundamental tones by adding tubing. Refer to Figure 8.1, which shows a diagram of rotary valves compared to piston valves.

The French horn in F uses written "C" (concert "F") as its fundamental to produce open tones (Fig. 9.8).

The French horn is fingered with the left hand so the fingering charts will be the reverse from those of the other brass instruments. See Figure 9.9 for the basic F horn fingering chart.

Figure 9.7.   French horn.

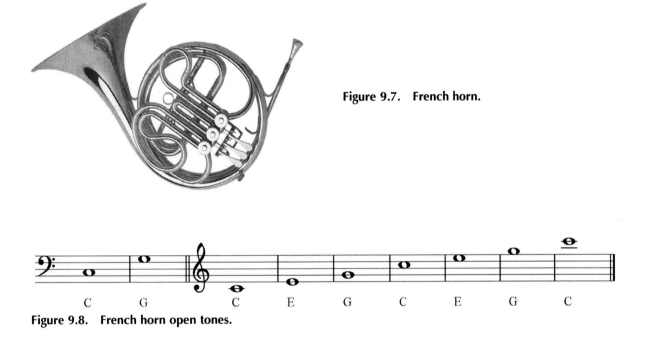

C   G   C   E   G   C   E   G   C

Figure 9.8.   French horn open tones.

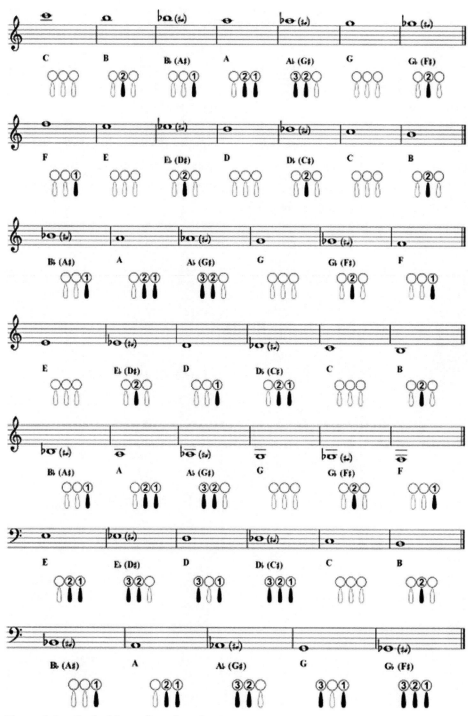

Figure 9.9.   Basic F horn fingering chart.

Basic B♭ French Horn Fingering Chart

Because its open tones are farther apart (Fig. 9.10), the B♭ French horn uses F as its fundamental (see Figure 9.11 for the fingering chart) and is easier to play.

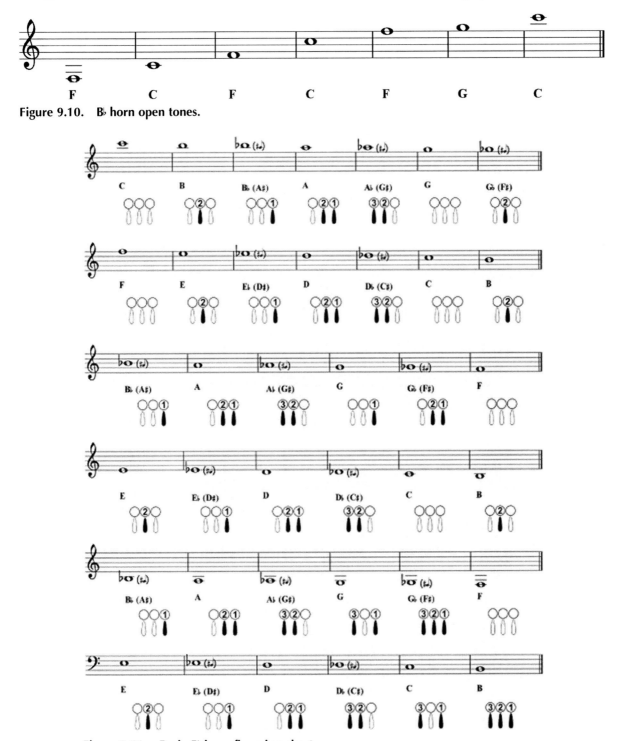

Figure 9.10. B♭ horn open tones.

Figure 9.11. Basic B♭ horn fingering chart.

Double Horn in F and B♭

The double horn is a single horn in F with a fourth valve used to open a B♭ crook (additional tubing) to make a double F–B♭ instrument (Fig. 9.12). By pressing a thumb trigger, the player can switch from a horn in F to a horn in B♭. This enables the player to more easily play notes with close interval proximity that present difficulties in tone placement. The trigger is required to achieve accuracy in five of the open tones below, in effect, making them not exactly open tones (Fig. 9.13). The fingering chart is shown in Figure 9.14.

Figure 9.12.   Double horn in F and B♭.

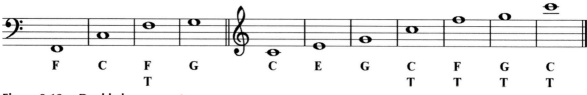

Figure 9.13.   Double horn open tones.

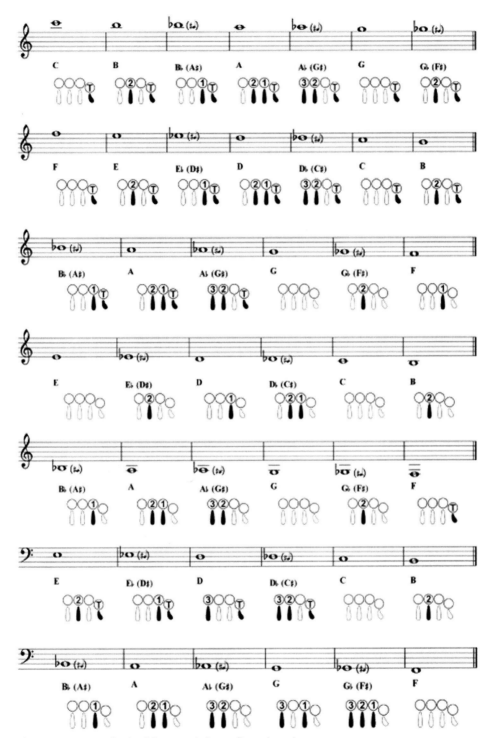

Figure 9.14. Basic double French horn fingering chart.

Tenor Trombone

The tenor, or slide, trombone in B♭ (Fig. 9.15) uses a slide to produce the tones between the fundamental and its upper partials. Figure 9.16 shows the tones that can be produced with the slide in its uppermost first position.

Figure 9.15.   Tenor trombone.

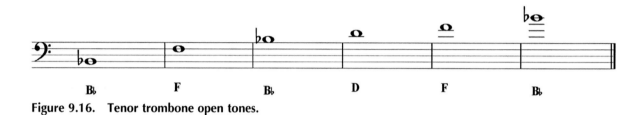

B♭   F   B♭   D   F   B♭

Figure 9.16.   Tenor trombone open tones.

To play the tones between the open tones, extend the slide in half-step increments. The approximate distances the slide must travel for each position are as shown in Figure 9.17.

First position: closed
Second position: 2.5 inches
Third position: 6.5 inches
Fourth position: 8.25 inches
Fifth position: 13.5 inches
Sixth position: 19 inches
Seventh position: 24 inches

The slide trombone is the only brass instrument that can be played in perfect tune because the slide can be placed at any point necessary to achieve accurate intonation. (See Figure 9.18 for the position chart.) All valve instruments are subject to the pitch inaccuracies that are inherent in the design of the instrument.

The valve trombone has the appearance of a trombone except that there are three piston valves built into the slide design and the slide portion is stationary (Fig. 9.19). The

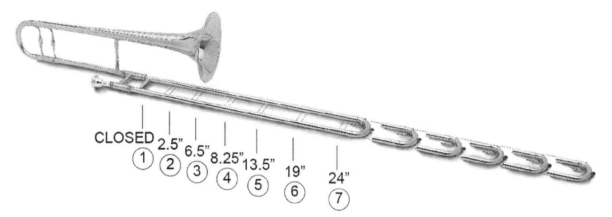

Figure 9.17.   Basic tenor trombone position diagram.

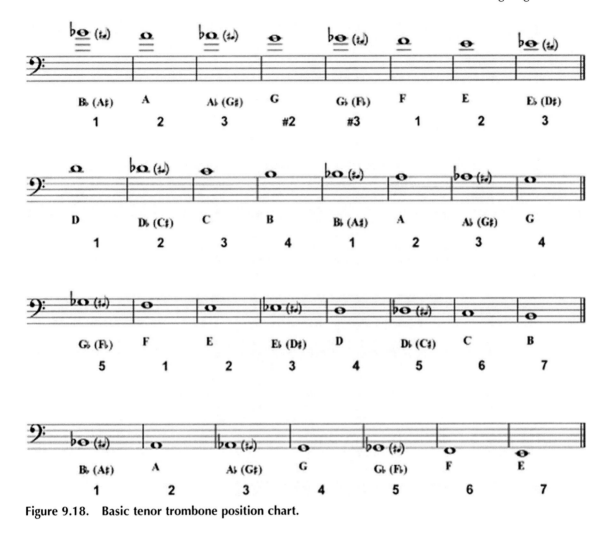

Figure 9.18.   Basic tenor trombone position chart.

primary use of the valve trombone is to facilitate a lower brass player in doubling on the trombone. The valve trombone uses the same fingering (Fig. 9.20) as the baritone horn in bass clef and the euphonium.

Figure 9.19.   Valve trombone.

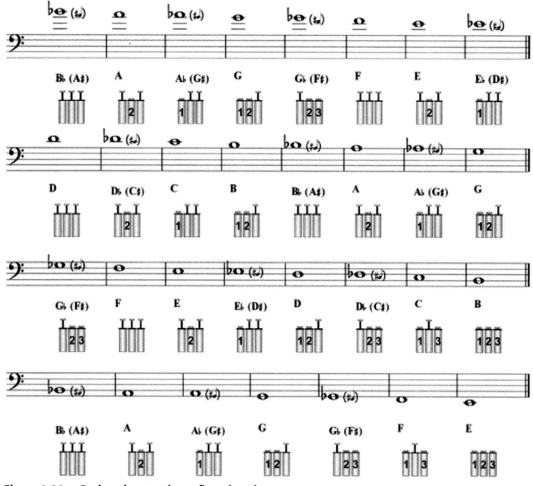

Figure 9.20.   Basic valve trombone fingering chart.

Mellophone

The mellophone (Fig. 9.21) resembles a French horn in sound and is used as a substitute when an actual French horn is not practical or available. It is useful when a quick change from the trumpet or cornet to a French horn–like instrument is required. The mellophone is produced in two designs, one for marching and a second duplicating the shape of the French horn.

The instrument is played with piston valves located for use with the right hand, is available in E♭ and F, and uses the same fingering as that of the trumpet (Fig. 9.22).

Figure 9.21.   Mellophone.

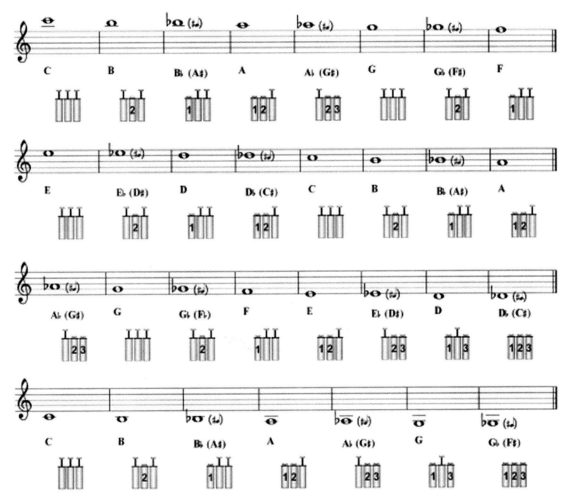

Figure 9.22.   Basic mellophone fingering chart.

Alto Horn

The upright E♭ alto horn (Fig. 9.23) is primarily a marching instrument and is often used in place of the French horn. Easy to carry, this instrument has a brassy tone and predominantly functions as a support to the rhythm section of the marching band.

The alto horn is made in E♭ only and shares the same fingering as that of the trumpet (Fig. 9.24).

Figure 9.23.   Alto horn.

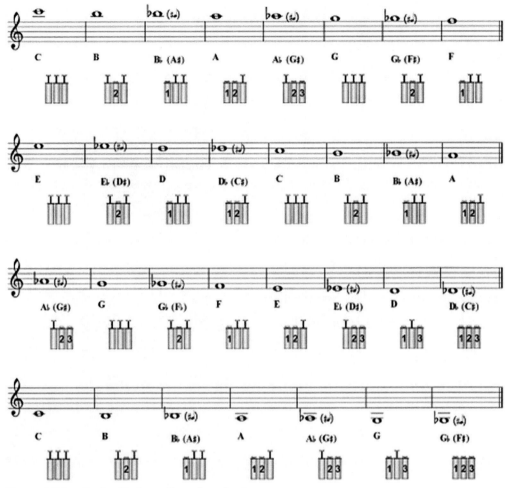

Figure 9.24. Basic alto horn fingering chart.

Baritone Horn

The baritone horn in B♭ (Fig. 9.25) can be played in both the treble and bass clef. When played in the treble clef, the baritone horn becomes a transposing instrument like the trumpet and uses the same fingering as the trumpet (Fig. 9.26). This allows for easy doubling for trumpet players. When played in the bass clef (Fig. 9.27), the instrument is non-transposing and shares the same fingering as the euphonium (Fig. 9.28) and valve trombone.

A form of tenor or baritone horn producing a rich mellow tone due to its large bell and bore, the euphonium (Fig. 9.29) is best left to perform slow lyrical bass solos. Like the baritone, it, too, is built on the B♭ overtone series and shares the same bass clef fingering chart.

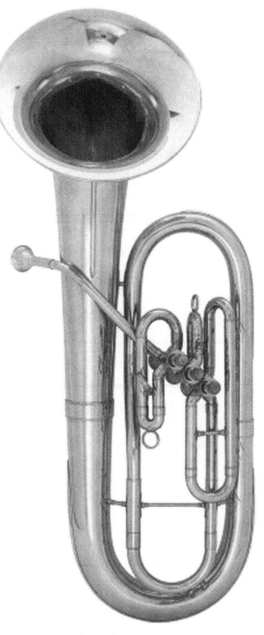

Figure 9.25.   Baritone horn.

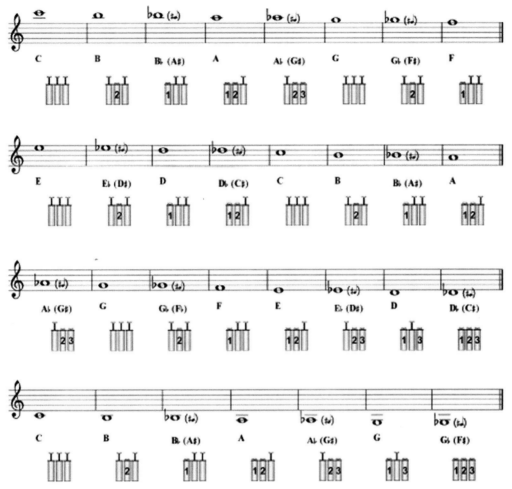

Figure 9.26. Basic baritone horn treble-clef fingering chart.

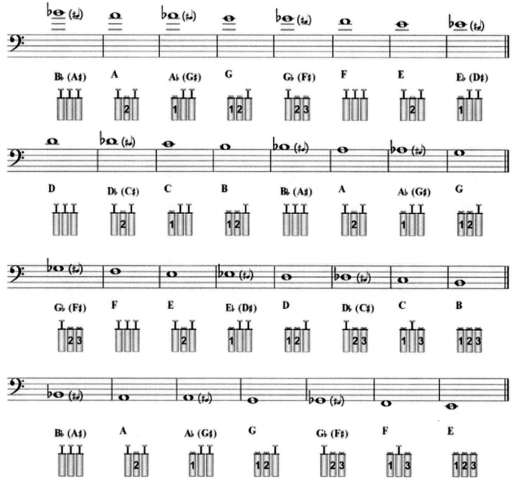

Figure 9.27. Basic baritone horn bass-clef fingering chart.

Figure 9.28. Euphonium.

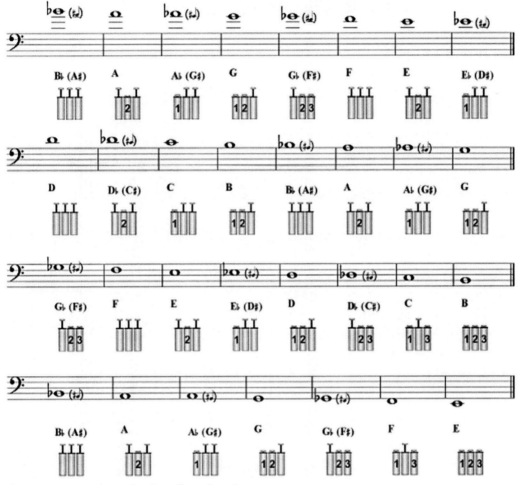

Figure 9.29.   Basic euphonium fingering chart.

Tubas and Sousaphones

BB♭ tubas (Fig. 9.30) and sousaphones (Fig. 9.31) are built with three and four valves in either piston or rotary design. The upright bell model shown in Fig. 9.32 is primarily used for concert work. A similar instrument with a bell facing front called the recording model tuba is used for marching.

In addition to the upright and bell front BB♭ tubas is the sousaphone. The instrument was named after the historic band master and composer of military marches John Philip Sousa. This instrument was designed for marching but can also be placed on a stand for concert use. The fingering chart for a B♭ tuba is shown in Figure 9.33, and the one for an E♭ tuba is shown in Figure 9.34.

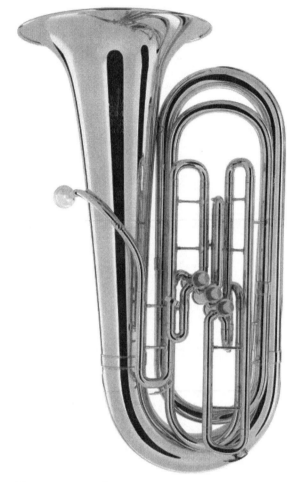

Figure 9.30.   Tuba.

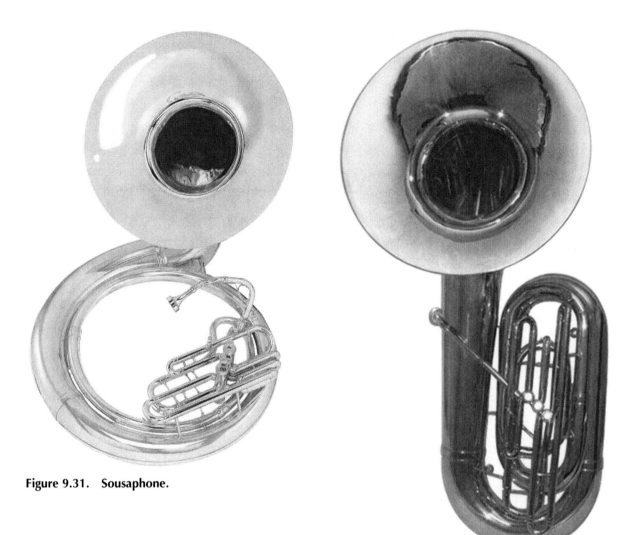

Figure 9.31.   Sousaphone.

Figure 9.32.   Recording model bell front tuba.

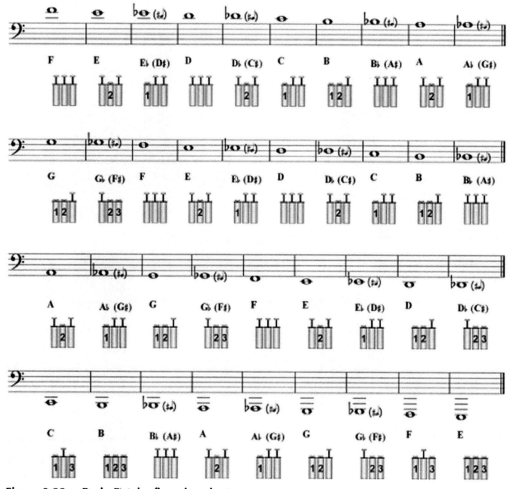

Figure 9.33.   Basic B♭ tuba fingering chart.

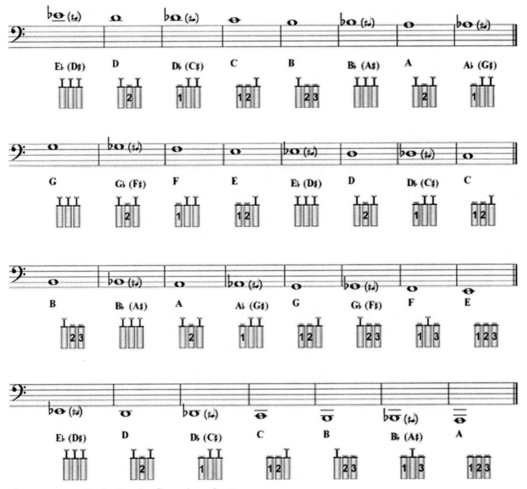

Figure 9.34. Basic E♭ tuba fingering chart.

Chapter 10

Brass Instruments

Expanded In-Depth Study

The names of brass instruments contain three terms that describe the kind of instrument, its practical performance range, and the overtone series upon which its acoustical design is based. An example would be the soprano trumpet in B♭, a (1) trumpet that plays in the (2) soprano range with a fundamental overtone series (i.e., without the use of valves) in (3) B♭.

Among the brass instruments currently in use are families of trumpets, trombones, French horns, tenor and baritone horns, and tubas. Each of these families is made up of an assortment of instruments of a similar design and size with variations primarily in the range, transposition or fundamental, and timbre. Presently, manufacturers produce a large assortment of trumpets, flugelhorns, cornets, trombones, alto horns, mellophones, tenor horns, euphoniums, baritone horns, tubas, and sousaphones.

Producing a Tone

To produce a tone on a brass instrument, the player buzzes her lips into a cup-shaped mouthpiece. The upper lip produces the primary buzz. Depending on the embouchure of the player, the lower lip buzzes to a lesser degree. The lower lip also acts as a support or stabilizer for the vibration of the lips and controls the size of the opening through which the air passes into the mouthpiece.

Every conceivable opinion on the placement of the mouthpiece on the lips has been offered by experts. The only point of agreement is that the placement is unique to each embouchure and must ultimately be determined by the player.

The fundamental pitches produced on a brass instrument can be altered by increasing or decreasing the intensity of the buzz. This is accomplished by raising or lowering the corners of the mouth. Pulling the corners of the mouth down will raise the pitch, and raising the corners of the mouth will lower the pitch.

113

Selecting a Mouthpiece

Since the size, shape, and structure of embouchures differ, the user must resort to prudent selection of the mouthpiece. The following general principles of brass mouthpiece construction will help in the mouthpiece selection process.

1. Each player has a unique dental and lip structure that creates a unique embouchure. It follows that each player needs a unique mouthpiece in order to produce the best possible sound.
2. Each instrument must have a mouthpiece that matches the design dimensions of that particular instrument, especially in relation to the size of the instrument's bore.
3. The mouthpiece's inner dimensions are critical to its output and must be matched with the player's needs and the bore of the instrument.
4. Mouthpiece model numbers and letters indicate the size of the various parts of the mouthpiece. Low numbers indicate larger cup diameters.

High numbers indicate smaller cup diameters. Models without letters following the numbers have medium-deep cups producing a full, rich, deep sound. "A" cups are very deep; "B" cups are medium; "C" cups are medium shallow; "D" cups are shallow; "E" cups are extremely shallow; and "W" models have a wide cushion rim for thick, soft lips.

When selecting a mouthpiece, evaluate the player's physiological characteristics and the instrument's structural requirements. Then determine the level of proficiency of the player, and finally, the nature of the player's performance needs. On the basis of this information, determine what combination of mouthpiece components will serve the player best.

It is essential that the player tries a number of mouthpieces that approximate the proportions that have been decided on as appropriate. In the final analysis, the response of the mouthpiece to the player's embouchure should determine the choice.

The Anatomy of a Mouthpiece

A brass mouthpiece consists of six parts. Figure 10.1 shows a cross section of a trumpet mouthpiece. The parts shown are the rim, cup, shoulder, throat, backbore, and shank.

All brass mouthpieces have these components. The factor that distinguishes them from each other for the different instruments is the size of their components and, therefore, the overall size of the mouthpiece. The design

of a tuba mouthpiece is similar to all other brass mouthpieces, but it is sized to fill the acoustical requirements of that instrument.

The effectiveness of a mouthpiece is the result of the combination of its components in conjunction with the player's lips or embouchure. The totality of these factors ultimately becomes the sound generator.

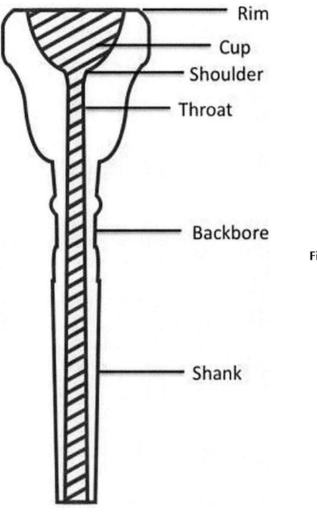

Rim
Cup
Shoulder
Throat

Backbore

Shank

Figure 10.1.   Brass mouthpiece image.

The Mouthpiece Rim

The rim of a mouthpiece is the part that comes into contact with the player's lips. The size and shape of the rim are generally described as being wide, narrow, round, or sharp (Fig. 10.2).

When selecting a mouthpiece, the first consideration must be the shape of the rim in relation to the player's embouchure. Since the rim size and shape profoundly affect the player's tone quality and endurance, it is important that the player select a rim that is best suited to his lip shape and size. The most effective width of the rim is usually similar to the lip size. Most players will need a medium rim. Players with thick lips would most likely benefit from using a wide rim, while players with thin lips should use a narrow rim.

Although a reasonable degree of comfort is desirable, priority must be given to the sound generation response that the player will obtain from the rim selected. The size and shape of the rim that produces the best sound, not the one that feels best, should be the one chosen.

Cup size

 Large cup diameter produces a large volume, reduces the risk of cracking tones.

 Small cup diameter requires little strength. It limits the tone, inhibits embouchure development.

Cup depth

 Shallow cup designed for higher pitched instruments, makes playing in the upper register easier.

Deep cup improves the tone, especially in the lower register.

Rim shapes

 Wide rim increases the player's endurance, but also limits flexibility

Narrow rim enables player to cover a wide range of pitch

 Round rim – A player with irregular dental structure may require a rounded rim contour. However, this is at the expense of clean low-register attacks.

 Sharp rim edge produces a brilliant metallic tone, makes attacks more reliable.

Figure 10.2.   Brass mouthpiece parts chart.

The Mouthpiece Cup

In the structure of the mouthpiece, the rim is followed by the cup (Fig. 10.2). The factors to consider in choosing the cup are its diameter and depth. The diameter provides the area in which the player's lips vibrate, so a diameter that is too small might restrict the vibration. Using the widest diameter possible will allow the player's lips more vibrating space and thereby permit a fuller sound.

The depth of a cup follows the principle of acoustics, which permeates all of musical instrument design. The larger the instrument, the deeper and more mellow the sound. Deeper cups favor lower sounds, whereas shallower cups favor higher sounds.

The Shoulder

The shoulder of the mouthpiece is the door to the throat (Fig. 10.1). The shoulder controls the flow of air into the throat of the mouthpiece and in so doing greatly affects the tone

quality. Again, selection must be predicated on the embouchure of the player. The size that allows the player to produce the best sound with the least effort would be the best choice.

The Throat

The throat of the mouthpiece (Fig. 10.2) also follows the general acoustical principles of size-to-pitch relationship (i.e., larger instruments favor lower sounds and vice versa). It is, therefore, necessary for the player to choose a mouthpiece throat size that will best serve the other components selected for the mouthpiece in question. Bear in mind that, since the throat controls the air flow, too small a size will tend to smother or mute the extreme registers, while too large an opening will not provide sufficient control to result in the optimum tone.

The Backbore

The backbore (Fig. 10.2) of the brass mouthpiece is the column that follows the throat. This portion of the mouthpiece is not generally considered in terms of size but rather in terms of its shape. The backbore starts out at the throat at its (the backbore's) narrowest and then enlarges as it reaches the end of the shank. Larger spaces produce deeper and louder sounds, while narrower or smaller spaces restrict the flow of air, offering more resistance and favoring higher sounds.

The Shank

The shank (Fig. 10.2) of the mouthpiece is the portion that enters the mouthpipe of the instrument. It is essential that the shank make perfect contact with the inside of the mouthpipe in order to avoid a leak or space that would cause turbulence in the flow of the vibrating air column.

Material

Another consideration in evaluating brass mouthpieces is the materials from which they are made and the effects those materials have on tone production and playing ease. Sterling silver, German nickel silver, silver- or gold-plated brass, plastic, Lucite, aluminum, and stainless steel are the materials most commonly used. There are as many opinions as there are players about which is best, but sterling silver, silver plate, and nickel plate are by far the most popular.

One additional option available in the selection of mouthpieces for brass instruments is the detachable rim that screws on and can be used with mouthpieces of various components. With a screw-on rim, a player can switch mouthpieces when doubling on an instrument other than the player's usual instrument and not have to adjust to a different rim. The screw-on rim also allows the player to switch to a Lucite rim when playing outdoors in cold weather. This is particularly convenient because the player can avoid using a metal rim, which can freeze onto the lips.

The number of possible combinations of mouthpiece components can be expressed mathematically as seven factorial (7!) since seven different parts can be combined. This means (multiplying 7 by 6 by 5 by 4 by 3 by 2 by 1) that there are 5,040 possible combinations of mouthpiece components. Good luck!

Chapter 11

Brass Instruments

Functioning

The Sound Voyage

The sound produced by a player buzzing into the mouthpiece of any brass instrument sets into motion the body of air that is present in the instrument. The player's breath sets her lips buzzing. That motion is then transmitted to the air column contained within the tubing of the instrument. When that air column is set into motion, sound is heard. The sound is then altered by the player's lengthening or shortening the tubing by one of several mechanical means to be discussed later in this chapter.

The immediate flow of air from the player's lips does not necessarily travel through the instrument to exit the bell end as a sound. When a player initiates a buzz into a BB♭ tuba, a sound occurs immediately in spite of the fact that the player's breath does not have time to travel throughout the entire instrument to produce that sound. It would take several full breaths to fill up the tubing of the instrument before any air could reach the bell. The sound is caused by the buzzing of the player's lips exciting the air existing in the instrument.

Tone produced on a musical instrument contains not only one pitch but a fundamental pitch plus a series of sounds called upper partials or overtones. The natural order of upper partials contains an inherent problem of diminishing interval relationship. The higher the interval in the harmonic structure, the closer is the tonal relationship of the two notes creating the interval.

Brass instruments' use of the upper partials increases in number as the instrument rises in its relationship to its family members. A tuba uses open tones that are farther apart from each other than those of the French horn. This being the case, a problem of inconsistency of intonation arises, which is inherent in all brass instruments. The intervals that occur higher up on the overtone series will be smaller in size by a small fraction than the same interval taken from a lower point in the overtone series (Fig. 11.1).

Therefore, an interval of a second between the twelfth and thirteenth partials, for example, E–F♯, would be smaller than one between the

Figure 11.1. Brass instrument upper partials.

tenth and eleventh, G–A. Since most tones played on brass instruments are harmonics, they are, by their very nature, not true in pitch and so the brass player's problems begin.

The bore of brass instruments is often a subject of disagreement and misinterpretation. It is said, for example, that the trumpet has a cylindrical bore while the cornet has a conical bore. In fact, neither is entirely the case. Brass instruments use a combination of conical- and cylindrical-shaped tubing to form the body and mechanism of the instruments. The leadpipe, valve, and bell section of brass instruments each require a different shape and size in order to function in a prescribed manner (Fig. 11.2).

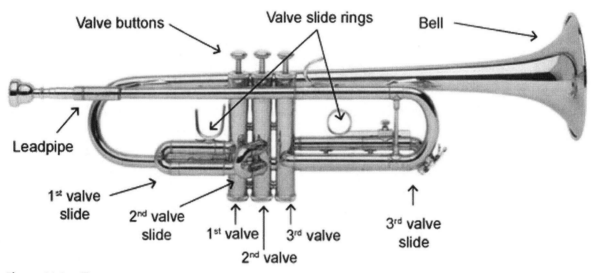

Figure 11.2.   Trumpet parts.

Most often, the bore size of brass instruments is referred to as being either large, medium, or small. There is no industry standard for the exact dimensions of these categories, so, when the terms are used, the interpretation of their meanings must be judged in a broad sense. It is generally accepted that the larger the bore size, the deeper the sound. Large-bore instruments produce a Teutonic sound, medium bores permit more flexibility for the player, and small bores produce a brighter, crisper sound.

Valves and Slides

In order to produce all of the chromatics that occur between the open tones on a brass instrument, the length of the instrument must be altered. To achieve this, the design of the instrument must in some way facilitate the availability of seven different lengths of tubing for the player to use at will. This is accomplished by a system of piston or rotary valves that open ports leading to additional tubing or by a slide, such as is found on a slide trombone, which lengthens the instrument's vibrating column thereby lowering the pitch. These mechanisms are not at all complicated or intimidating in appearance.

The trombone slide is the simplest of systems and the most reliable in providing the

Trombone Slide Mechanism

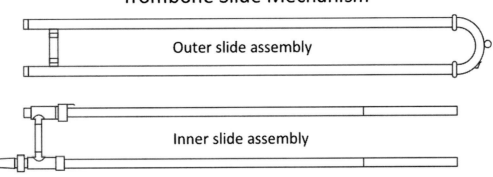

Outer slide assembly

Inner slide assembly

Figure 11.3. Trombone slide mechanism.

performer with the opportunity to produce accurate intonation. Since the player is able to place the slide anywhere within its range, complete control of the length of the vibrating air column is available and, therefore, so is complete control of intonation. For this reason, the slide trombone offers the best opportunity for playing a brass instrument in tune (Fig. 11.3).

Conversely, valves restrict the player because a valve can only be fully depressed or fully released with no options in between. The result is a myriad of intonation complications that are virtually insurmountable. When the player depresses a piston valve, the holes in the piston are realigned, extending the length of the tubing—called a valve slide section—associated with that valve (Fig. 11.4).

The rotary valve serves the same function as the piston valve, but instead of traveling up and down like the piston, the rotary valve turns in its casing. When the valve rotates, it realigns its ports to open new valve slide sections. This increases the length of the vibrating column of air lowering the pitch (Fig. 11.5). Rotary valves are most commonly used on French horns and less commonly on tubas and trumpets.

Although both types of valves produce the same result, they differ in their response.

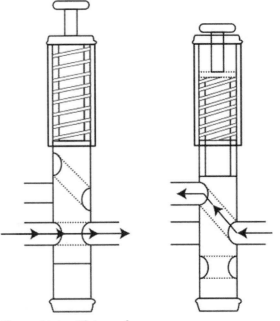

Figure 11.4. Piston valve.

Piston-type valves must be depressed by the player without any sideward pressure in order to be effective. Failure to depress the piston valve in a true vertical direction will result in its scraping on the interior wall of the valve casing, decreasing the effective accuracy of the piston.

Rotary valves are considered by many to be easier to use, allowing the player greater agility. In the design of trumpets using the rotary valve system, the placement of the first valve is about two inches from the mouthpipe instead of the usual ten inches as on a piston-

Rotary Valve Mechanism

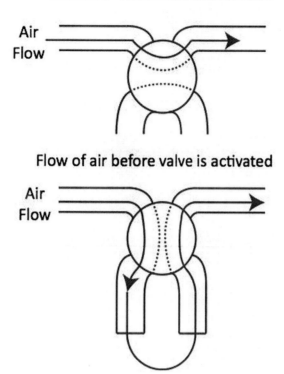

Flow of air before valve is activated

Redirected flow after valve activated

Figure 11.5.   Rotary valve.

valve design. This structural difference results in a less accurate scale in pitch production along with some loss of brilliance.

On all brass instruments, the valves, regardless of type or design, serve the same function. The first valve lowers the fundamental tone being produced by the player by one full step. The second valve lowers the fundamental by one half-step, and the third valve lowers the fundamental by one-and-one-half steps (Fig. 11.6).

The theory is quite simple to understand. Unfortunately, these simple mechanical processes create a potpourri of acoustical complications, which have to date remained the nemesis of the brass player.

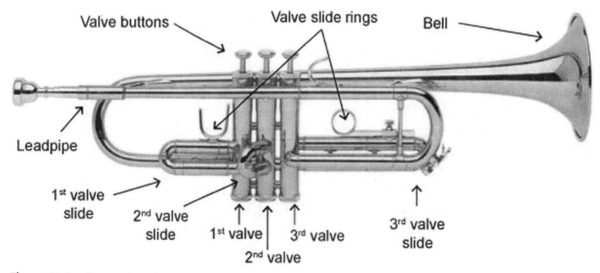

Figure 11.6.   Trumpet parts.

Intonation

Intonation difficulties occur because occidental (Western) music uses the tempered scale intended for keyboard instruments, whereas brass instruments are built to produce the natural, or just, scale, the result of the natural harmonic series of overtones. As these two scales approach their extreme ranges, the comparative frequencies differ, so that open G5 (a step above the fifth line in the treble clef) on the trumpet produces a pitch that is higher than that same note on the tempered scale.

An even greater problem of intonation arises when the valve systems are activated. Recall that the second valve lowers the fundamental by one half-step, the first valve by two half-steps, and the third valve by three half-steps. When the second valve is depressed on a trumpet, the instrument is converted from its natural B♭ overtone series to an A overtone series. This creates, in effect, a new instrument, a trumpet in A instead of in B♭. A trumpet in A is longer than a trumpet in B♭ and, therefore, requires longer tubing for the first and third slides, if the ratio of these slides is to remain consistent with the new length of the instrument. Of course, the first and third slides do not change, so, when additional valves are activated in conjunction with the second slide, intonation begins to fail.

There are two problems: the just scale versus the tempered scale, and the distorted ratios incurred by the use of the valves. These can be compensated for but not totally corrected by the manufacturer's selecting a midpoint in the length of the valve slides to ease the problem of pitch and provide the least possible inaccuracy of pitch under all conditions.

In addition to that compromise, many brass instruments are fitted with valve slide rings, allowing the player to quickly and easily adjust the length of the particular slide in use at that moment (Fig. 11.6).

As stated previously, the mechanics of valve instruments are not particularly complex. Simply, a piston, a rotor, or a slide does the job. Unfortunately, two of these three systems, namely, the rotor and the piston, do not offer the performer an opportunity to play her instrument in perfect tune, but instead create problems of intonation that do not exist on the original brass instruments before valves are added. Conversely, without valves the user is limited to the overtone series as performed by embouchure changes. It is obvious that the addition of valves is the lesser of the two evils.

Annotated List of Brass Instruments

The following is an annotated list of the more common contemporary brass instruments.

Trumpet

The trumpet's effective sound-producing and amplification system begins with a cup-shaped mouthpiece usually made of brass, coated with silver. The mouthpiece is inserted into a slightly conical-shaped tube called a mouthpiece receiver, which in turn is connected to the main body of the instrument. The major portion of the trumpet is cylindrical and contains the cylinders that house the valves. The valves can be either of the piston or rotary type. Following the main cylindrical section of the instrument is the bell section. This is again conical in shape and is about one quarter the length of the preceding cylinder.

The trumpet is designed with a tuning slide for each valve. Presently, the following list of trumpets is being manufactured and used most commonly: mezzo-soprano in C and B♭; soprano in D; high E♭; high F; sopranino in high G; piccolo in high B♭; contralto in low E♭ and F; and tenor in C and B♭.

Cornet

While the trumpet is primarily cylindrical with some conical parts, the cornet is almost totally conical. Sharing essentially the same design principles as the trumpet, the cornet begins with a cup-shaped mouthpiece somewhat smaller than that of the trumpet. This is connected to a lead pipe, which joins the remainder of the body of the instrument.

The overall appearance of the instrument is shorter than the trumpet because the tubing is usually bent into two loops. The combination of the smaller conical bore and the two turns in the tubing present greater resistance to the player, with the resulting tone being mellower than that of the trumpet. Currently in use are the mezzo-soprano cornet in B♭ and soprano in high E♭.

Flugelhorn

This instrument is, in effect, a bass trumpet. It has the same range and pitch as the trumpet but demonstrates its unique characteristics in the contralto range, where it produces a tone that has a rich, mellow timbre. The instrument is available in mezzo-soprano in B♭ and bass in B♭.

French Horn

French horns are manufactured in B♭, F, and a combination of the B♭ and F horns, called a double horn. Using a double horn, the player can switch from B♭ to F by pressing a thumb trigger, which turns a rotary valve to redirect the vibrating column of air from one section of tubing to another. Switching from F to B♭ enables the player to avoid playing the high notes that depend on upper partials of the overtone series. Due to their close interval proximity, these notes present difficulties in tone placement.

The (single) French horn in F consists of a coiled tube approximately 76 inches long. The addition of the B♭ crook to create a double horn increases the length by 52.5 inches. The total length of the combined F-B♭ (double) horn becomes 10 feet, 8.5 inches.

The single horn in F contains three rotary valves, which open and close the various lengths of tubing. The double horn has a fourth valve. This operates the B♭ crook added to the single horn to make a double F-B♭ instrument.

The bore of the instrument beyond the valves is conical up to and including the bell, which ends in a diameter of around eleven inches.

The Mellophone

The mellophone resembles a French horn and is used as a substitute for the horn when an actual French horn is not practical or available. The instrument is played with piston valves located for use with the right hand. The mellophone is useful when a quick change from the trumpet or cornet to a French horn–like instrument is required. Mellophones are constructed in E♭ and F.

Slide Trombone

The slide trombone is the only brass instrument that can be played in tune. This is so because instead of valves, the trombone uses a slide to lengthen or shorten the instrument. If the player is capable of discerning proper pitch placement, there is no limit to the level of pitch perfection attainable since the slide can be placed at any point necessary to achieve accurate intonation.

Due to the slide design, the bore of the instrument must be primarily cylindrical. The exception occurs with the taper of the bell section, which flares out to approximately eight to nine inches at the widest point. This section of the instrument is equal to about one-third of the entire length of the instrument.

Trombones come in an assortment of models, among which are the alto in E♭, tenor in B♭, symphony in B♭, bass in B♭, valve in B♭, and trombonium in B♭.

Valve Trombone

This instrument has the appearance of a trombone except that there are three piston valves incorporated into the slide design and the slide portion is stationary. The primary use of the valve trombone is to facilitate a lower brass player in doubling on the trombone. Because of the valves these trombones suffer the same intonation problems as do other valve instruments.

Alto Horn

The upright E♭ alto horn is primarily a marching instrument and is often used in place of the French horn. Easy to carry, this instrument has a brassy tone and is predominantly used as a support to the rhythm section of the marching band. The alto horn is made in E♭ only.

Tenor Horn

More commonly used in central Europe, the tenor horn, so named for its range placement in the scheme of brass instruments, is used for solo passages that require more virtuosity than those normally associated with instruments in the lower range. The tenor horn is built in the key of B♭.

Baritone Horn

Representing the baritone voice in the brass family, the instrument is less versatile than the B♭ tenor horn and has a more mellow voice. The baritone horn is used most often in American concert bands and is built on the B♭ overtone series.

Euphonium

A form of tenor or baritone horn producing a rich, mellow tone because of its large bore, the euphonium is best left to perform slow lyrical bass solos. Like the baritone horn, the euphonium is built on the B♭ overtone series.

Tuba

The tuba, the lowest of the brass instruments, comes in several designs. The upright bell is used primarily for concert work while the recording model, or bell front model, is used for marching. In addition, there is the famous tuba designed for marching known as the sousaphone.

Tubas are built with three and four valves in either piston or rotary design. The various models available are the rotary or piston valve in BB♭ and CC, three valve in BB♭ and E♭, four valve in BB♭, and sousaphone in BB♭ and E♭.

Marching Band Instruments

A complete line of brass instruments called marching band instruments exists. These are identical to the instruments mentioned above in function, except that they are designed to be held in a horizontal playing position, as you would hold a trumpet, in order to facilitate playing while marching.

Summary

The manner in which brass instruments function acoustically, mechanically, and musically is almost identical. The materials from which they are made are the same. They all use the player's lip buzzing into a cup mouthpiece, coupled with a brass body as an amplifying system fitted with valves that are used to extend the length of the body of the instrument. The slide trombone is the exception. Unfortunately, this family of instruments also shares the characteristics, again with the exception of the slide trombone, of having inherent intonation problems.

The intonation problems begin with the sound generator being the human lips functioning as a buzzing device. Through this system of sound generation, the brass player is restricted to the limitations inherent in her own lip and mouth configuration. The brass player does not have the option of changing the components of the tone generator as do other instrumentalists. Single-reed players can change mouthpieces, reeds, and ligatures. Double-reed players have their reeds made to order or make them themselves. String players have a vast variety of strings, bows, and bridge configurations at their disposal. Brass players can change but not modify their mouthpiece of choice.

Whereas all other instrumentalists can select components with which they can customize their sound generators, brass players are born with theirs. The only outside assistance they can turn to is the cup mouthpiece. There are numerous mouthpiece designs available to accommodate the infinite number of shapes of lip-mouth configurations. Ultimately, however, brass players, unlike woodwind instrumentalists, cannot simply change their reeds.

The second problem that is unique to brass instruments, again with the exception of the slide trombone, is the change in valve-slide ratios as the pistons are depressed. Devices such as the valve slide trigger and the addition of a fourth valve on some instruments, along with some creative concepts in bore construction, all have helped to improve the intonation problems. However, it is apparent that the valve system used on brass instruments at best provides an inexact system of intonation.

Listeners have adjusted to these imperfect sounds by sheer exposure, tending to accept the sound of the brass section as being a product of timbre rather than of imperfect intonation. In fact, they have become accustomed to it and consequently find it acceptable. Of all the problems with instruments in use at this time, the brass player's plight is the most difficult in the area of intonation. Good intonation on a brass instrument must rest with the ability of the performer to humor individual notes as required by each situation.

The brass choir provides the power and brilliance essential to the performance of band and orchestral music, as it evolved with the works of Beethoven, Brahms, and Wagner during the Romantic period. Military, cere- monial, and entertainment bands could not fill their roles without the brass choir's dynamic character. So, as is the case with anything we love and need, we accept it for its virtues and live with its imperfections.

Chapter 12

Non-fretted String Instruments

Easy-Reference Quick Start

This chapter provides an overview of the violin, viola, cello, and double bass, also known as non-fretted string instruments or the violin family.

The Instruments

The violin, viola, cello, and double bass (Fig. 12.1), the four instruments of the string family, are very similar in their design, acoustics, and construction. As a result, they share many playing techniques and fingering patterns.

Figure 12.1.   Violin family.

How They Work

Using Figure 12.2 as your guide, when a string (1) is set into motion, its vibration is conducted by the bridge (2) to the top of the instrument (3), transferred via the soundpost (4) to the back (5) and distributed laterally throughout the top by the bass bar (6). The top and back are supported by the sides (7). The combined motion of these parts sets the air contained within the body of the instrument into a pumping motion that forces the resonating sound out of the instrument through the "f" holes (8). The purfling (9) controls the vibration of sound throughout the top and back while reinforcing the structure of those two parts of the instrument.

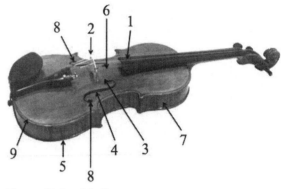

Figure 12.2.   Violin parts.

The Bow

Violin, viola, cello, and double bass bows are very similar in design, construction, and use patterns (Fig. 12.3). The differences are in size and in the shape of the frog. The violin frog (A) is squared off at the back. The viola bow (B) is slightly larger in all dimensions and has a rounded edge on the back of the frog. The cello bow (C) is still larger than the viola bow in all dimensions and also has a rounded edge on the back of the frog. The double bass uses two different types of bows, the French style and the German style.

The French bass bow (D) has the same design as that of the viola and cello but is much larger than either. The German bass bow (E) sports a grip-type frog and is held in the palm of the hand with the fingers on the top, side, and bottom of the frog. A more detailed description of how these bows are held will follow under sound production.

A bow made of pernambuco wood and strung with horsehair is the bow of choice. A more cost effective and practical choice for

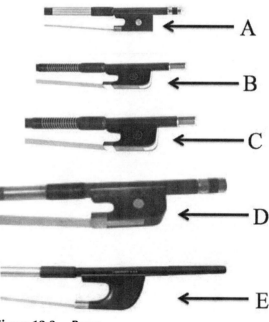

Figure 12.3.   Bows.

beginning students is a bow made with a fiberglass stick and fiberglass hair or, if possible, horsehair. The fiberglass bows are much less expensive, very durable, and are considered by most teachers of beginning students to be a very adequate substitute for the more expensive wood/horsehair combination.

Figure 12.4 is a diagram showing how the hair is installed on a bow. More on this will be discussed in the In-Depth section to follow.

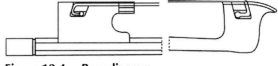

Figure 12.4. Bow diagram.

The Process of Tuning

The violin, viola, and cello all have wedge-shaped wooden pegs, which are forced into holes in the peg box. These instruments require the same tuning procedure.

1. For the violin and viola, hold the instrument on your lap with the scroll up and the strings facing you. For the cello, hold the instrument on its end pin on the floor with the strings facing you.
2. Using a piano, pitch pipe, or electric tuner, select the correct pitch for the string you are tuning.
3. When you have the pitch firmly fixed in your mind, pluck the string to be tuned. The next step is vital to successful tuning.
4. While the string is sounding the note you have just plucked, slowly tighten the string by turning the peg toward the top of the scroll, and, as you turn the peg, push in so that it is forced into the holes of the peg box (Fig. 12.5). Please note that if you do not force the peg into the peg holes, the peg will not hold the string in tune.
5. While you are slowly turning and pushing the peg in, listen to the sound of the string getting higher. When it reaches the pitch you have in mind, stop. The string will be tuned.

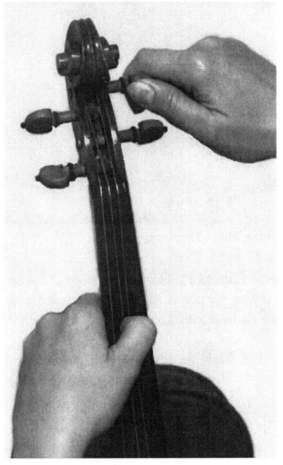

Figure 12.5. Tuning.

6. If necessary, you can further adjust the pitch in small degrees by tightening or loosening the fine tuner (Fig. 12.6).

Due to the greater thickness of the strings, the double bass uses a worm and gear system to tune its strings and to keep them in

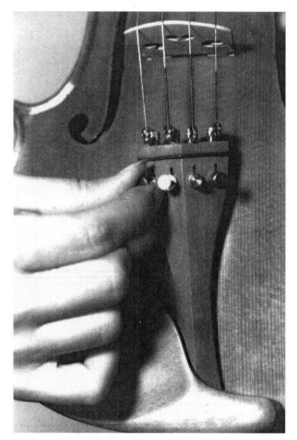

Figure 12.6.   Fine tuning.

Figure 12.7.   Worm and gear system.

tune (Fig. 12.7). This system merely requires turning the peg in the direction needed with no pushing action.

1. Hold the bass in playing position.
2. Using a piano, pitch pipe, or an electric tuner, select the correct pitch for the string you are tuning.

3. When you have the pitch firmly fixed in your mind, bow the string to be tuned. Due to the lower pitched strings on the double bass, bowing rather than plucking will produce a sound more easily heard for tuning purposes.
4. While the string is sounding the note you are bowing, turn the machine gear peg up or down as needed.
5. When the sound reaches the pitch you have in mind, the string will be tuned.

Experienced players can further fine tune their instrument through the use of harmonics. By bowing the string being tuned and touching it at a spot about mid-way down the string, the player can break the vibrating pattern and produce a falsetto-like note that is easier to hear and permits a more refined pitch adjustment. The operative word in this paragraph is "experienced." It takes a bit of practice to perform this procedure effectively.

The Open Strings

The strings on the violin, viola, and cello are tuned in fifths. The double bass is tuned in fourths. Starting from the lowest string, the instruments are tuned as shown in Figure 12.8

(violin), Figure 12.9 (viola; movable C clef represents middle C), Figure 12.10 (cello), and Figure 12.11 (double bass; one octave below the written notes).

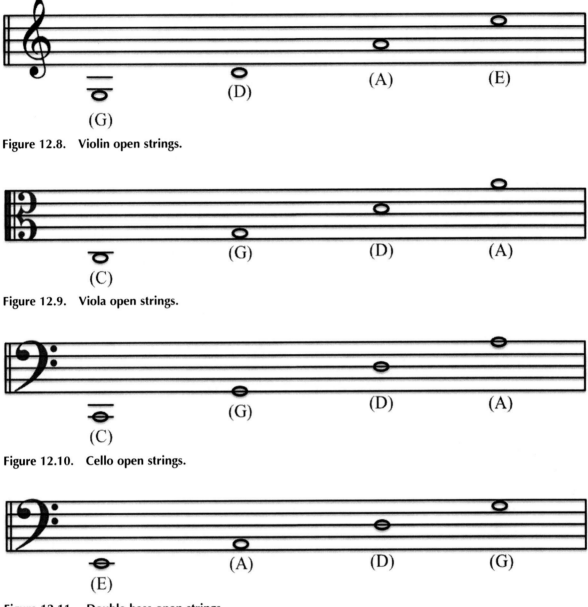

Figure 12.8. Violin open strings.

Figure 12.9. Viola open strings.

Figure 12.10. Cello open strings.

Figure 12.11. Double bass open strings.

Fingering

The traditional introduction to fingering on any instrument usually begins with one note at a time as an individual topic. A fingering chart illustrating all of the fingering for all the notes in the range of the instrument being studied is also provided.

Using this approach the student rarely realizes that every instrument has a simple, repetitious pattern that, when understood in its totality, significantly facilitates determining fingering for all notes on all the instruments in that choir.

The fingering patterns for the violin, viola, and cello are almost identical. The player is able to raise the pitch of each string in half steps or in any interval up to seven steps above the open string by depressing the string to the fingerboard with the fingers of the left hand (Fig. 12.12).

Figure 12.12.   Fingering.

Playing Position

Playing position refers to the placement of a player's fingers on an instrument's fingerboard in relation to the open string. The chart in Figure 12.13 is a guide to these labels for the violin and viola. Placement of the first finger above the position names the open string.

The patterns for the violin and viola are the same except for the distance between the fingers. The distance between each finger can be adjusted to produce either a half step or whole step. Adding fingers adds steps. Adding multiple fingers produces intervals.

Fingering for the cello follows the same pattern except that there is a half position for every full position. The pattern is as follows: ½, 1, 2, 2½, 3, 3½, 4, 5, 5½, 6, 6½, and

Placement of first finger above the open string	Position name
Half step	Half
One step	First
One and a half steps	Second
Two and a half steps	Third
Three and a half steps	Fourth
Four steps	Fifth
Five steps	Sixth
Six steps	Seventh

Figure 12.13.   Intervals.

7. Each of these positions progresses by half steps up to the seventh position. Note that whereas the violinist and violist can play five half steps in each position the cellist can only play three half steps. There are no half positions for the first and fourth positions because of the natural half step between E and F and B and C in the diatonic scale.

Fingering for the double bass follows a slightly different pattern because its larger size requires a greater spread between notes and because the ring finger is not used alone but is used in conjunction with the pinky. Used individually, they both generally lack strength. The pattern for the positions on the double bass, starting from an open string is: ½, 1, 2, 2½, 3, 3½, 4, 5, 5½, 6, 6½, 7. Each of these positions progresses by half steps up to the seventh position. Note that the double bass player is restricted to playing only three half steps in a position because the third and fourth fingers are used in combination. There are no half positions for the first and fourth positions because of the natural half step between E and F and B and C in the diatonic scale.

Fingering Charts

For the charts in this section, press the string at the position noted on the chart, using the fingers indicated at the left, to finger a note. See Figure 12.14 for the basic violin fingering chart, Figure 12.15 for the basic viola fingering chart, Figure 12.16 for the basic cello fingering chart, and Figure 12.17 for the basic double bass fingering chart.

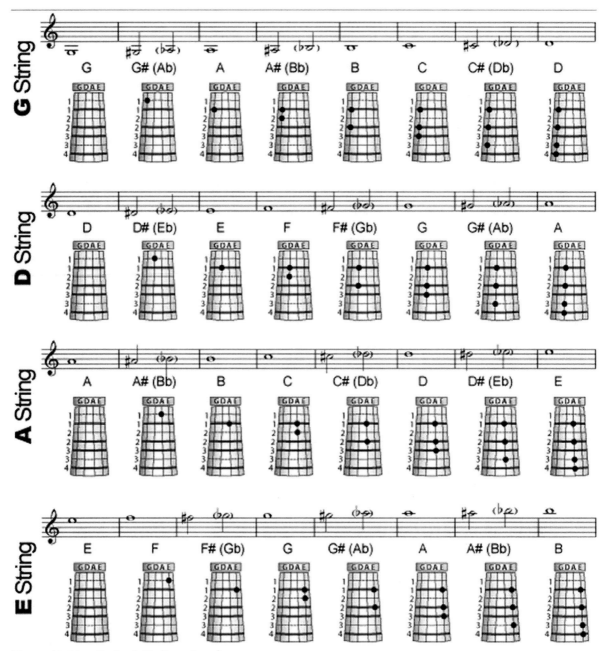

Figure 12.14. Basic violin fingering chart.

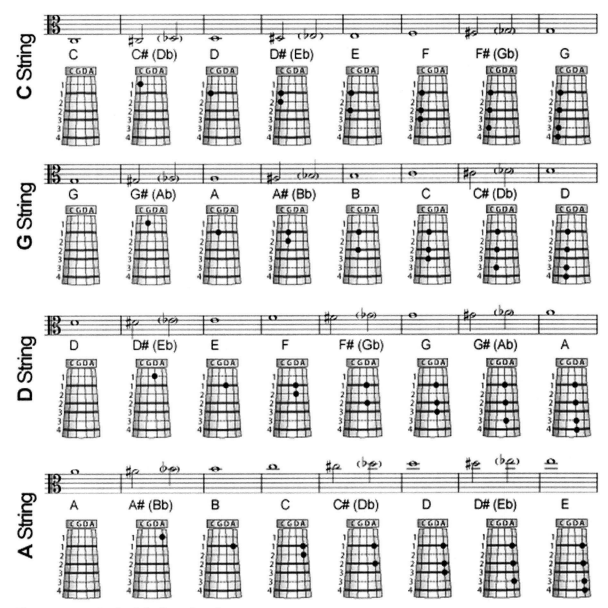

Figure 12.15.   Basic viola fingering chart.

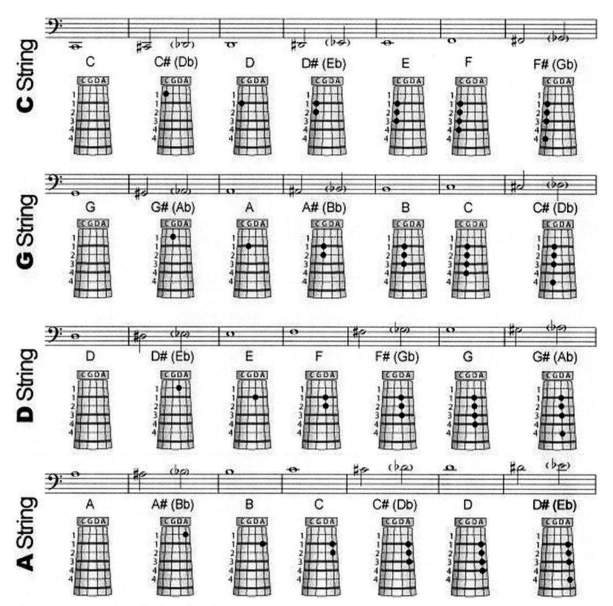

Figure 12.16. Basic cello fingering chart.

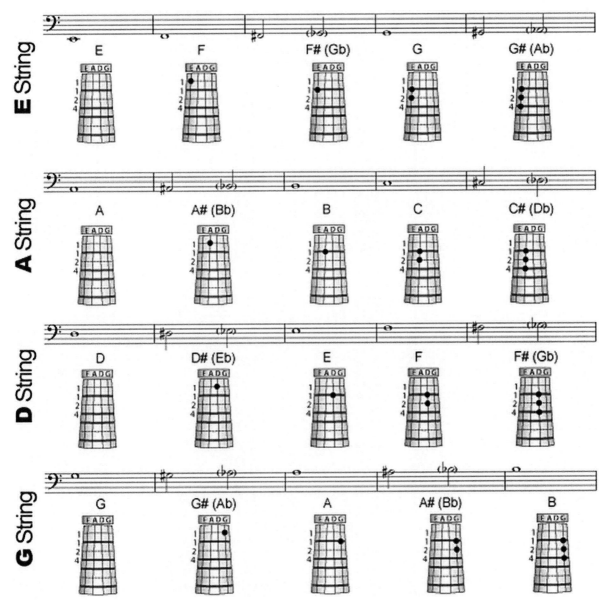

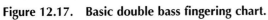

Figure 12.17. Basic double bass fingering chart.

Chapter 13
Non-fretted String Instruments
Producing Sound

The method most often used to produce a sound on a non-fretted string instrument is drawing a wooden bow strung with horsehair across a string (Fig. 13.1).

Figure 13.1. Violin playing position.

Holding the Bow

The following are some recommended ways to hold a bow. The final position arrived at for holding a bow or for playing any instrument becomes the result of the individuality of the player's physical makeup and the position that is most effective and comfortable for the player. Note the violations of all rules at the next live performance you attend.

1. With your left hand, pick up the bow by the center of the stick with the frog facing your right hand.

2. Bend your right thumb in at the first knuckle and position your thumb between the hair and the stick with your thumb gently pressing into the bow grip (Fig. 13.2).

3. Rest your index finger at the first knuckle on the opposite side of the stick and slightly forward of your thumb.

4. Allow your pinky finger to fall naturally, with a slight arch, on the screw end of the bow. The exact point where you are able to balance the bow will be the correct placement for each individual. The thumb, index finger, and pinky finger are the three fingers that control the balance of the bow (Fig. 13.3).

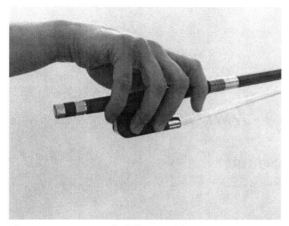

Figure 13.2.   Bow holding position.

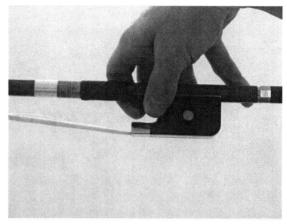

Figure 13.3.   Bow holding position.

5. Allow your middle and fourth fingers to fall naturally on the outer side of the stick.

6. While holding the stick in this manner, adjust your finger positions to that which will allow you to have best control over the bow.

This description applies to the violin, viola, cello, and French style bass bows. The German style bass bow (Fig. 13.4) has a frog that requires a grip different from the other bows. For the German bow, hold the bow by the stick with your left hand and place the frog in the palm of your right hand with the screw extending between your thumb and index finger. Place your thumb around the top of the bow stick and your pinky finger on the underside of the frog. Allow your middle and ring fingers to comfortably grip the inside of the frog.

Each grip will be individual. Strive to adjust your grip in such a manner as to have complete control of the bow with a firm yet relaxed hold (Fig. 13.5).

As stated previously, a pernambuco wooden bow with horsehair is the bow of choice. A more cost effective and practical choice for beginning students is a bow made with a fiberglass stick and fiberglass hair or, if possible, horsehair. This topic will be discussed more fully in the next chapter.

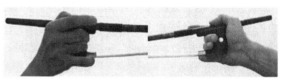

Figure 13.5.   German bass bow holding position.

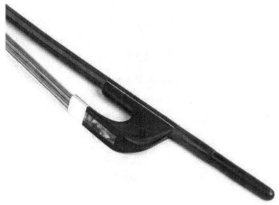

Figure 13.4.   German bass bow.

Strings

Among the most common products used to make strings are gut, steel, perlon (a type of plastic fiber), silk, chromium/steel, and gold. Each type of string construction produces a different sound quality and can alter the overall tone quality of an instrument. The choice of strings, therefore, becomes a matter worthy of great consideration.

For beginning students, the most practical and cost effective strings would be steel or perlon because they stretch the least (which allows them to maintain their pitch) and are less likely to break. This topic will be discussed more fully in the next chapter.

Chapter 14
Non-fretted String Instruments
Expanded In-Depth Study

The family of non-fretted string instruments, often referred to as the family of violins (Fig. 14.1), consists of the violin, viola, cello, and double bass. These instruments form a string choir that covers a range of around five and a half octaves. Just as choral music uses the soprano, alto, tenor, and bass voices, so the string choir uses the violin, viola, cello, and double bass, respectively.

The unique characteristic of the family of violins is that they are all constructed using the same design, acoustical principles, and manufacturing techniques. Instruments of the woodwind and brass choirs also have

Figure 14.1. Violin family.

similarities within their respective groups, but they do not begin to approach the close relationship that the violin family shares. All four use the same process for initiating, amplifying, and manipulating sound.

Structural differences among these instruments, aside from their size and playing range, are slight. The violin is the most acoustically perfect of the four. The viola, cello, and double bass are progressively (but not proportionately) larger while still maintaining essentially the same structure and design of the violin; however, their acoustical perfection does wane as their sizes increase.

The viola is often described as being a large violin because both instruments share many characteristics of design, physics, construction, and appearance. The instrument is tuned a fifth lower than the violin but is one-seventh larger, making the difference in pitch disproportionate to the difference in size. This ratio of tuning to size results in the darker timbre associated with the viola.

While the body of a full-size violin is almost always the same size, 14 inches (35.5 centimeters) long, the size of a viola body can vary as much as four inches. Viola body sizes can range from 13.5 inches to 17.5 inches in length with the widths ranging proportionate to the length.

Another difference appears in the size-to-pitch ratio. An instrument that is tuned a perfect fifth below the violin should be considerably larger than the viola, if it were to follow the size-to-pitch ratio set by the design of the violin. In fact, the size of the viola should be so great that it would not be manageable as an instrument to be played under the chin. Since the size of the viola is not correctly proportioned to its tuning, viola makers can enjoy a bit of latitude when de-

signing the instrument, and can alter the size to produce the tone quality desired.

The cello, or violincello, is also disproportionate in size to its difference in tuning. It is tuned a full octave below the viola but is smaller than its acoustical requirement. The discrepancy is compensated for by a significant increase in the depth or thickness of the body of the instrument. With the increased depth, the lower tones are able to resonate with the characteristic timbre of the cello. Due to its relatively large size, the cello is supported by an end pin that extends from the bottom of the instrument (Fig. 14.2). The end pin is adjustable in order to accommodate players of varying sizes.

Figure 14.2.   Cello end pin.

The cello rests with its end pin on the floor, while the player balances the instrument between the knees. In this position, the strings are reversed from their positions on the violin and viola. In playing position, the lowest string, the C string, now becomes the first string on the right hand of the player; this is in opposition to the playing position of violins and violas, which have the highest string at the player's right side.

The double bass is the lowest-sounding instrument of the violin family. Although it, too, shares the principles of the string instrument design, the double bass has the greatest structural differences of the family.

As stated previously, double bass pegs are not made of wood nor do they function on the wooden wedge principle. Because of the greater thickness of the strings, there is need for a stronger and more stable peg treatment. This necessity produced the worm and gear system now used exclusively on this instrument (Fig. 14.3).

Figure 14.3. Double bass worm and gear system.

This system can also be used on fretted string instruments and can be installed on any of the other three instruments of the violin family. Such a modification is usually restricted to use on student instruments, since the worm and gear mechanism helps facilitate the tuning of a string instrument. Unfortunately, this mechanism adds a considerable amount of weight to the peg box, so the ad-vantages of easier tuning are outweighed by a possible problem of balance on the violin or viola. The use of the worm and gear system is more practical on the cello and the double bass, since the instrument rests on the floor and balance is less of a burden to the player.

In addition to its larger size, the double bass differs slightly in shape from the violin, viola, and cello. While the shoulders of these instruments are at a ninety-degree angle from the fingerboard, the size of the double bass requires that the shoulders be sloped in order to allow the player to reach the higher playing positions comfortably (Fig. 14.4).

Figure 14.4. Double bass shoulders.

Another difference is found in the back of some double basses. Rather than being rounded, the back of the larger instrument starts out from the heel of the neck sloping outward and then levels off to a flat back for the major portion of the instrument (Fig. 14.5). This design allows the maker to use less than half of the wood required for a rounded back without sacrificing any structural integrity.

Some double basses have a fifth string, enabling the performer to play down to C a third below the lowest string on the instrument. An additional way to achieve this extended range is by installing a device that lowers the pitch of the fourth string to C.

Figure 14.5.   Double bass back.

Construction

All the instruments in the violin family are constructed using the same design, acoustical principles, and manufacturing techniques. The violin, the most acoustically perfect of the four, will be used as a model for a study of the entire family of non-fretted string instruments.

The viola, cello, and double bass are progressively (but not proportionately) larger while still maintaining essentially the same structure and design of the violin.

The violin is a model of simplicity composed of shaped wooden wedges, plates, and strips, which support the strings and permit the player to shorten the open strings in order to raise the pitches from the original tuning.

Figure 14.6 is a diagram of the violin naming the exterior parts. The mechanism that supports the strings consists of the scroll

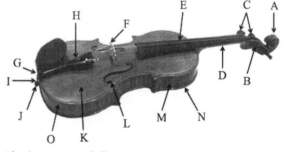

Figure 14.6.   Violin parts.

(A), peg box (B), pegs (C), neck (D), fingerboard (E), bridge (F), saddle (G), tailpiece (H), tailgut (I), and end button (J). The body of the instrument is made up of a top (belly) (K), "f" holes (L), sides (ribs) (M), a back (back plate) (N), and purfling (O) surrounding the top and back plates. These parts form the exterior of the body.

Inside the instrument (Fig. 14.7), supporting the exterior of the instrument are the ribs (A), top and bottom block (B), corner blocks (C), bass bar (D), and soundpost (E).

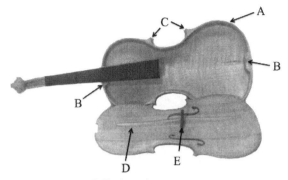

Figure 14.7.   Violin interior.

Materials

The materials most commonly used for the construction of violins are spruce, maple, ebony, and rosewood. The top of the violin is generally made of spruce since it is a softer wood and fills the design description for the most effective sound amplification. Spruce is also used for the soundpost, linings, and the bass bar.

The back, sides, gluing blocks, neck, and scroll are generally made of hard maple, again in compliance with the prescription for achieving the most responsive amplifier while maintaining structural integrity. Hard maple or a wood of similar strength is needed for these parts in order to support the tension exerted by the strings stretched across the instrument.

As shown in Figure 14.8, the end button (A), saddle (B), tailpiece (C), fingerboard (D), nut (E), and pegs (F) are usually made of

Figure 14.8.   Violin parts.

ebony, rosewood, or, in the case of low-quality instruments, less expensive hardwoods, metal, or plastic.

All of the instruments of the violin family are constructed of the same materials and essentially use the same technology in practically the same manner. The only difference will be found in the size and proportions of the larger instruments. In the construction of less expensive larger instruments, laminated wood is used to cut costs while improving the structural integrity of the instrument.

There are two ways in which wood can be cut for use to make the upper and lower plates (top and back) of the violin. If it is the intention of the maker to construct an instrument with a two-piece back plate, the wood is cut into a triangular-shaped block, which is then cut vertically down the middle to form two triangles (Fig. 14.9). These are then joined to form one plate that is subsequently carved into shape. This process is used in order to increase the likelihood of achieving a symmetrical wood grain pattern.

The second possibility is to cut a layer of wood that will produce a one-piece plate. This method eliminates the seam from the middle of the plate (Fig. 14.10). The disadvantage of

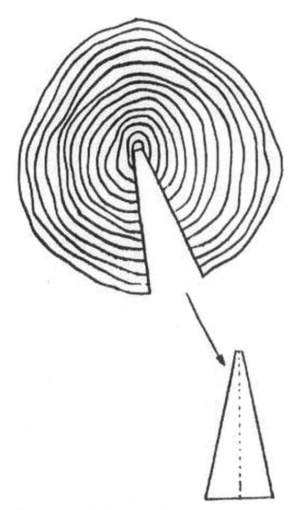

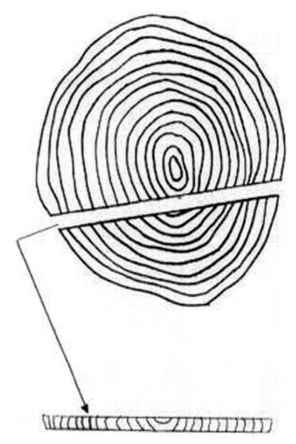

Figure 14.10.   Cross-cut wood cut.

Figure 14.9.   V-shape wood cut.

this method is the likelihood that a one-piece slab of wood, because of the span of the size required, will have a variation in grain as the cut progresses. It is most desirable to maintain a uniform grain in the production of these plates. The triangle cut maintains this uniformity because the cuts are taken from a smaller portion of the overall slab of wood.

The Bow

The bows used to play the instruments of the violin family are strung with horsehair or fiberglass hair substitute. Figure 14.11 illustrates how the stick of a bow is strung. A hank of horsehair (A) is selected and combed so that all hairs are parallel to each other. The end of the hank is then tied and wedged securely into a box-shaped cutout (mortise) at the tip of the bow (B). The hair is held in place by a wooden, wedge-shaped plug (C) that is accurately cut to exactly fit the space remaining in the cutout box. This plug holds the hair in place.

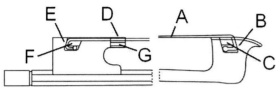

Figure 14.11.   Bow diagram.

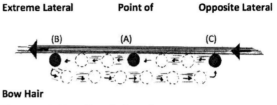

Bow Hair
Figure 14.12.   Bow hair string contact.

A ferrule (metal band) (D) is inserted over the hair, which is carefully drawn along the bow, tied at the end, and inserted into a similar box-shaped cutout in the frog (E). Again, a wooden, wedge-shaped plug is placed into the box (F) to secure the hair in place. Finally, a slide and another wooden wedge are inserted between the ferrule and the frog (G) to help distribute the hairs equally and laterally and to keep them in place.

About Horsehair

When viewed with the naked eye, horsehair appears to be smooth, but under examination with a microscope, the surface of the hair is quite rough. Particles, called follicles, project from the hair, forming an abrasive surface.

Rosin, a tree sap derivative, is applied to bow hair to increase its gripping power. When rosined bow hair is drawn across a string on an instrument, the hair grips the string and excites it into motion causing the vibration that produces a tone.

As a bow is drawn across a string, the bow hair appears to be in constant contact with the string. However, this is not the case. The bow hair is actually gripping and releasing the string in a rapid sequence replicating a plucking action. This action causes the string to be drawn to a point where its lateral tension is sufficient to overcome the gripping force of the rosined bow hair (Fig. 14.12).

When it reaches that point, the string releases itself from the bow and returns to cross its point of equilibrium, proceeds to its opposite lateral extreme, only to be gripped again by the bow hair and then to repeat the process.

The final effect is one of a string being gripped by the bow hair, pulled to a point of tension, breaking free from that grip, rebounding to a point opposite the point from which it was just released, and then being caught again by the bow hair, only to repeat the process. All of this occurs in such rapid succession that it is invisible to the naked eye.

Strings

A number of different materials are currently being used to manufacture strings. Among the most common are gut, steel, perlon (a type of plastic fiber), silk, chromium/steel, and gold. With the exception of the gold strings, all of the other products can be used as a core for strings that are then wound with aluminum, chromium, or silver. This process can be used for all strings except the violin "E" string, which, due to its high pitch, does not require the acoustical enhancement provided by wrapping.

Each type of string construction produces a different sound and can alter the overall tone quality of an instrument. The choice of strings, therefore, is a matter worthy of great consideration. It is possible to brighten or darken the tone quality of an instrument by selecting the string material that creates the desired effect.

When striving to achieve a particular tone, the user must evaluate the timbre of the instrument being strung and anticipate how that instrument will respond to each type of string. Unfortunately there are no prescriptions for making this determination; the performer must experiment to arrive at the combination of string and instrument that will satisfy her individual taste.

Although there are no concrete rules for selecting strings that will produce a particular sound, the following are some general guidelines that may facilitate the choice.

Steel or steel core strings are most durable, produce the most aggressive or brightest sound, stay in tune longer, and are generally prescribed for use by beginning players.

Gut strings usually produce a more mellow sound, but since they react to changes in temperature and humidity, they are most susceptible to pitch problems and tend to break more easily.

Gut core strings, which are wound with silver or aluminum, retain the characteristics of the pure gut but tend to have a fuller sound and somewhat greater durability.

Perlon, a nylon substance used as a core for wound strings, is stronger than gut, does not react greatly to temperature and humidity changes, and tends to stay in tune longer. Perlon strings produce a slightly more aggressive sound than gut strings.

The Bridge

When a bow is properly drawn across a string, the sound that is generated is conducted to the top, or belly, of the instrument by the bridge (Fig. 14.13). As the string vibrates, its transverse (side to side) motion is converted by the bridge into a perpendicular (up and down) "stamping" motion. The feet of the bridge transfer the vibrations by actually stamping on the belly of the instrument. Since the bridge plays a dominant role in transferring the sound from the string to the amplifier (body) of the instrument, the design and material used to make the bridge and its placement on the instrument must be calculated to fill that function in the best possible way.

The dimensions for string instrument bridges are unique to each instrument. Al-

Figure 14.13. Violin bridge.

though there are some guidelines for the initial cutting of the bridge (Fig. 14.14), the final product must be cut to fit the contour of the top of each instrument and to provide sufficient, but not excessive, height for the

INSTRUMENT	HEIGHT	THICKNESS TOP	STRING SPACING
VIOLIN	E 1/8" G 3/16"	1/16"	7/16"
VIOLA	A 3/16" C 1/4"	1/16"	1/2"
CELLO	A 1/4" C 5/16"	3/32"	5/8"
BASS	G 7/16" E 11/16"	3/16"	1-1/8"

Figure 14.14.   Bridge height chart.

strings to clear the fingerboard. The height of a bridge is measured as the distance it elevates the strings above the end of the fingerboard at two points—the highest and lowest pitched strings. The two intermediate strings are set proportionately following the contour of the end of the fingerboard. If the strings are proportionately set, the player will be able to bow each string comfortably without inadvertently bowing two strings simultaneously. Serious consideration must also be given to the spacing of the strings on the bridge so that they will span evenly over the fingerboard, starting from the nut and extending to the bridge.

The most common material used for bridge construction is hard maple. It is essential that the wood be hard, for it must withstand the pressure and friction of the taut strings. Sometimes inserts of even harder material are used (especially at the point on the bridge where the violin "E" string makes con-

tact) in order to withstand the cutting action of that very thin, taut string. Ebony, cowhide, rubber, or plastic are used in various ways to help prevent wear on the point of contact where the strings meet the bridge.

The placement of the bridge on the body of the instrument is crucial to obtaining optimum sound production. The feet of the bridge must be cut to fit the contour of the top of the instrument. The feet must then be placed so that looking from the tailpiece the left foot stands over the bass bar while the right foot stands slightly behind the soundpost, toward the fingerboard side. In this position the right foot of the bridge conducts the higher tones to the top of the instrument and on to the soundpost, which then carries the sound to the back of the instrument. The left foot conducts the lower tones to the bass bar, which transverses lengthwise along the instrument and distributes the sound across the top.

The Soundpost and Bass Bar

The soundpost (Fig. 14.15) plays an important role in sound transmission. In addition to acting as a structural support for the top of the instrument, this post, made of softwood, conducts

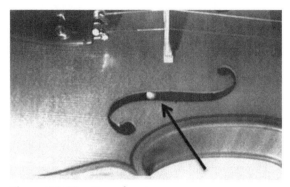

Figure 14.15.   Soundpost.

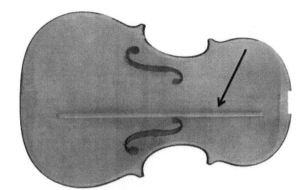

Figure 14.16.   Bass bar.

the vibrations from the top of the instrument to its back. The soundpost distributes tones produced by the higher strings to the back of the instrument, while muting any echo effect that would occur if that post were not present.

The bass bar (Fig. 14.16) serves two functions. Located on the underside of the top of the instrument, the bass bar reinforces the instrument, supporting the great force exerted by the tension of the strings. It also distributes the vibrations laterally throughout the top.

The soundpost and bass bar together distribute sound throughout the body, which acts as an amplifier for the sounds generated by the strings. The motion of the components stimulates the air pocket contained within the body into vibrating patterns of compression and rarefaction. The sound generated at the string is transported through the bridge, belly, soundpost, and bass bar to ultimately produce the tone of the instrument.

The Sides and Back

The function of the sides and back—in addition to enhancing the vibrating process—is to form the supporting structure for the entire instrument. The sides and back of the instrument, then, are made of a harder and thicker wood than the belly of the violin. A hardwood like maple is used most often and serves well as a support structure.

The tension incurred by the strings stretched from the top (pegs) to the bottom (tailpiece), some sixty-eight pounds (31 kg) for the violin, draws the top (scroll end) and bottom of the instrument (tailpiece end) toward each other. It is the strength of the back plate, with the aid of the sides, that prevents the belly (of a softer wood) from folding in half.

"F" Holes and Purfling

There are two parts of the sound amplifier that appear to be ornamental but, in fact, play an important role in the production of sound. These are the sound holes, or "f" holes,

so named because of their shape, and the purfling, which appears to be an ornamental trim inlaid around the edge of the top and back of the body.

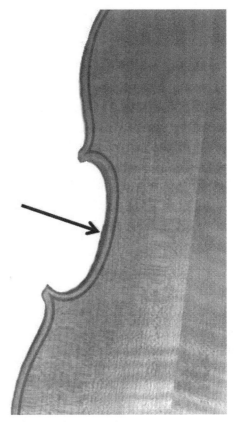

Figure 14.18.   Purfling.

Figure 14.17.   "F" holes.

The "f" holes (Fig. 14.17) significantly af-fect the quality of the tone of the instrument. The flexing action of the mid-portion of the top of the instrument, and the ability of the tone-saturated air within the sound box to escape, are affected by the size, shape, and lo-cation of the holes. Due to the importance of these shapely orifices, their exact shape, size, and location are distinctive to each craftsman.

Purfling (Fig. 14.18) is made of two par-allel strips of hardwood, usually ebony, which are inlaid into the surface around the edge of the top and back of the violin. Purfling serves an important acoustical purpose. The groove cut for the inlay acts as a barrier or interruption for the vibration that is travel-ing through the wood. Through the use of purfling, the maker is able to define clearly the area throughout which the vibration is to take place and thereby control that vibrating area and the tone it produces.

Summary

The complete amplifying process on non-fretted string instruments is shown in Figure 14.19. The string's vibrations (1) are conducted by the hardwood (usually maple) bridge (2) to the softer wood (usually spruce) top plate (3). The vibrations are then transported via the softwood soundpost (4) to the hardwood back (5) of the instrument, and via the softwood bass bar (6) laterally throughout the entire top.

Figure 14.19.   Violin parts.

The hardwood back and softer wood top (belly) are joined by hardwood sides (7). Combined, the top, sides, and back form an air space in which the sound circulates. The interaction of all of these components forms the amplifier for the sound produced by the strings. The combined motion of these parts sets the volume of air contained within the body of the instrument into a pumping motion that forces the resonating sound out of the instrument through the "f" holes. In this manner the instruments produce sound.

In spite of the more than three-hundred-year history of the violin, the exact interaction that takes place among these components is not yet fully understood. The mathematical simplicity and consistency of the design of the instrument becomes evident when one observes that violins hardly vary in their proportions.

The greatest amount of wood is found beneath the bridge. The thickness of the wood decreases to half the amount at the sides of the instrument while remaining consistent throughout the length of the bass bar. Farther across the top of the instrument, the measurement at the thinnest part of the top becomes equal to one quarter of the thickest part. The ratios then progress from the whole (thickest), to one-half of the whole (medium), to one-quarter (thinnest) of the whole.

The amplifier or body of a violin is deceptive in its simple appearance and yet it uses a most complex system for distributing vibrations. The vibrations are carried throughout the physical structure of the wooden body of the instrument and travel in every direction. This diversity of movement causes the instrument to vibrate and oscillate horizontally, vertically, and diagonally. Simultaneously, the air contained within the body is set into motion, increasing and decreasing in volume while traveling in and out of the body through the "f" holes.

The bodies of the woodwind and brass instruments' main functions are to contain the columns of air that are set into motion, and act as a structure into which various mechanical devices are incorporated to extend or shorten that vibrating air column. In the case of the violin family, the body acts as the amplifier of sound that profoundly affects the quality of tone produced and has no part in the changing of pitch. That, of course, is achieved by the player's fingers shortening (stopping) the strings.

An expertly crafted violin strung with an appropriate set of strings and played with a good quality bow will produce a better tone than a poorer quality instrument set up with the same bow and strings. Unlike wind instruments, the tone quality of string instruments is largely a product of the quality of the material used in the construction of the body of the instrument and of the design and craftsmanship used in making the instrument.

The violin, viola, cello, and double bass, sharing most of the same technology, combine to make the most versatile choir of instruments in the contemporary music world. These instruments share their design, acoustical function, construction, and history. They enjoy a romantic quality that has resulted in their being considered collectibles, works of art, a three-century-old mystery story, and the heart of the modern symphony orchestra.

Chapter 15

Percussion Instrument Overview

Percussion instruments produce sound by reacting to any type of agitation such as being struck, scraped, or, in the case of something with sound-producing particles in an enclosed vessel, shaken. By definition, then, almost anything can be labeled a percussion instrument. The result is that the percussion section is the largest category of musical instruments in the industry. For practical reasons, therefore, this chapter on percussion instruments will be restricted to those instruments that are most often found in traditional orchestras, bands, and other music-performing groups and will take the form of an overview instead of the quick start and in-depth format used in the preceding chapters.

Although percussion instruments play an essential role in most music groups, the instruments to be discussed in this section do not share the complexity in design, playing challenges, acoustical and sound generation characteristics, and mechanical intricacy that is found in a woodwind, brass, or string instrument. This is not to say that percussion instruments are not complex acoustical mechanisms. On the contrary, an in-depth look into the acoustics of many of these instruments would show a surprising degree of complexity. However, the objective of this manual is to introduce musical instruments to those who, for whatever reason, must deal with an instrument on which they are not proficient. Because of the vast variety of instruments that fall under the label of percussion instruments, to discuss their acoustical properties would be a task of such profound complexity that it would not serve the simple, succinct, easy-to-read, quick-study goal of this manual.

Classifications

Because of their wide variety in play today, percussion instruments appear in all of the categories of the classification scheme used in musical instrument study.

A broad classification used for percussion instruments is by the type of sound they produce. These are either tuned (definite pitched) as in a bell or timpani or not tuned (indefinite pitched) as in a snare or bass drum.

A more definitive set of classifications takes into consideration an instrument's sound-producing attributes. Called idiophones, chordophones, aerophones, or membranophones, these terms are used for all acoustical musical instruments.

Idiophones are instruments that, when activated by striking, rattling, scraping, blowing, rubbing, plucking, or any other form of instigation, produce sound through the vibration of the entire instrument. An example would be cymbals, bells, and chimes. When struck, these instruments respond with their entire structure to produce sound. Idiophones can be made of almost any material that can vibrate.

Chordophones in the percussion family are those instruments that use strings as their sound-producing source. In order for a chordophone to be classified as being in the percussion family, the strings must produce sound by being struck with a mallet or other hammer-like item. A hammered dulcimer or a piano is an example of a chordophone.

Aerophones are instruments that produce sound by a flow of air from any source. In the percussion family, whistles and sirens fall into that category.

Membranophones contain some form of membrane as part of their structure and produce sound when that membrane is struck or agitated in some way. Drums are membra-

nophones since they are constructed with a membrane stretched over a shell.

An additional unofficial category of percussion instruments is a catchall to cover the countless items that are not necessarily musical instruments but that can produce sound by any of the means described above and that are used in some manner in music performance. These would be items that fall into any of the four above-mentioned official categories, but with somewhat dubious justification for being called a musical instrument. Included would be anvils, pots and pans, and almost anything that will make a sound when agitated in any manner. The use of percussion instruments of this nature is most commonly found in twentieth-century contemporary or popular compositions. It is this catchall category that results in percussion instruments being the largest category of instruments in the field.

The unique position percussion instruments hold among their counterparts is that there is a large enough variety of them so that they appear in each of the four major musical instrument categories described above. Whereas woodwind and brass instruments are strictly aerophones and the violin family of instruments is strictly made up of chordophones, percussion instruments exist in every category.

The Snare Drum

A snare drum consists of a shell (Fig. 15.1) upon which a membrane called a head (Fig. 15.2) is attached on one or both ends. The head is attached with a rim (Fig. 15.3), which is bolted down to the shell with screws called tension rods (Fig. 15.4). These are screwed into threaded metal receivers, or lugs, connected to the shell. The tension rods can be tightened or loosened with a drum key (Fig.

15.5). Figure 15.6 shows the parts of the whole as they fit together.

Snares (Fig. 15.7) are curled metal or plastic wires stretched across the bottom head of the drum. This addition produces the rattle-like brilliance associated with the typical sound of a snare drum. The snares vibrate against the bottom head at each strike on the upper drum head. The upper drum head is

Figure 15.1.   Drum shell.

Figure 15.4.   Tension rods.

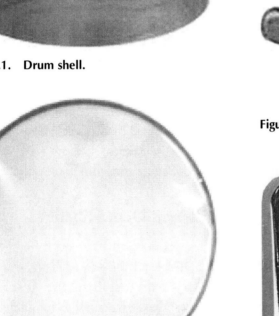

Figure 15.2.   Drum head.

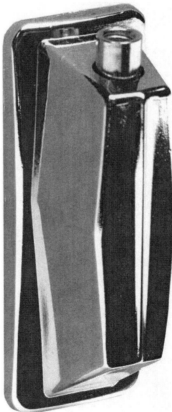

Figure 15.3.   Drum rim.

Figure 15.5.   Drum key.

Figure 15.6.   Snare drum parts.

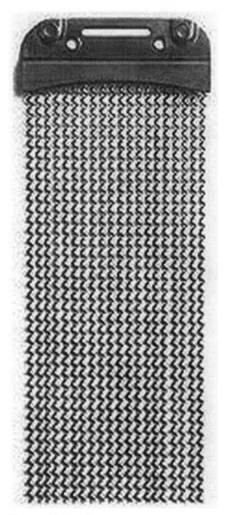

Figure 15.7.   Snare.

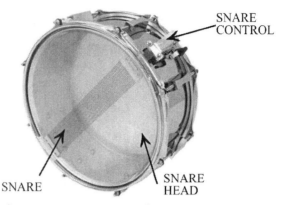

Figure 15.8.   Snare control.

called the batter head. The lower drum head is called the snare head (Fig. 15.8 and Fig. 15.9). Figure 15.9 shows an assembled snare drum and its parts.

Snares can be adjusted by means of a screw-tightening mechanism (Fig. 15.10) attached to the side of the drum. The snares can also be released by flipping a lever at the same location. Releasing the snare on a snare drum will result in a tom tom–like sound.

Different Depth Shells

Snare drum shells can be different depths, with the resulting sound being increasingly deeper as the depth of the shell increases. The standard size shell for a snare drum is between five and five and a half inches. A smaller drum called a piccolo snare drum is between three and four and a half inches

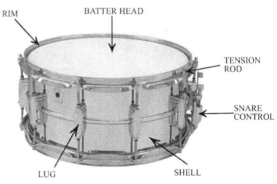

Figure 15.9.   Snare drum parts.

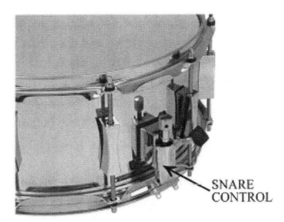

Figure 15.10. Snare release lever.

deep. A larger snare drum can be from six to ten inches deep (Fig. 15.11).

Tuning Procedure

The procedure used to tune a snare drum is essentially the same for all drums. The tension or tightness of the head will determine the nature of the sound produced. The head is tightened by turning the tension rods in a clockwise direction. To loosen the head, turn the tension rods in a counterclockwise direction (Fig. 15.12).

Adjusting the tension of the heads changes the sound produced and simultaneously changes the feel of the drum sticks as they strike the head. Tighter heads produce crisper,

Figure 15.12. Snare drum key.

higher-pitched sounds with a more resilient stick rebound. Looser heads produce mellower, lower-pitched sounds with a less resilient stick rebound. The choice is entirely up to the

3-4.5"   5-5.5"   6-10"

Figure 15.11. Different depth snare shells.

performer and should be determined by the type of selection being played and the venue in which the performance is taking place.

Tuning a drum head requires a bit more than just random tightening or loosening of the tension rods. In order to achieve balance, follow this procedure:

1. Release the snare by flipping the lever on the snare release shown in Figure 15.10.
2. With the head loose but securely in place with little but equal tension on the tension rods, depress the center of the head to ensure it is firmly seated on the shell. Be sure that all the tension rods are turned into the lug so that an equal amount of each tension rod is visible.
3. Select any tension rod as a starting point. Lightly tap the head with a drum stick approximately two inches from the rim opposite that tension rod and simultaneously tighten it to the degree where the head begins to show some resistance and the sound begins to change.
4. Repeat the process on the tension rod directly opposite the first one. Tighten that one until the sound being produced at that point on the head resembles the sound at the first.
5. Repeat the process on the tension rod next to the first one.
6. Repeat the process on the tension rod directly opposite that one.
7. Continue that procedure around the drum until all tension rods have been tightened to the degree desired.

On a six-lug drum, the tightening pattern of the tension rods should be 1–4, 2–5, 3–6 (Fig.

15.13). Over-tightening heads will reduce their productivity. The degree to which the tension of the batter and snare heads should match each other is an issue yet to be resolved. For a brighter sound, the snare head should be somewhat tighter than the batter head. The choice remains that of the performer.

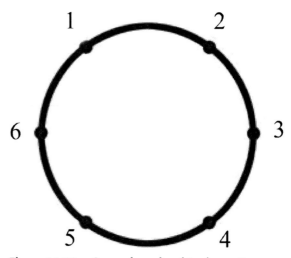

Figure 15.13.   Snare drum head tuning pattern.

This process can be used with both indefinite- and definite-pitched drums. The result to be achieved for indefinite-pitched drums should be to produce a percussive sound appropriate to the type of music to be performed. Definite-pitched instruments should be tuned to the pitch indicated in the music to be played.

There is a school of percussionists who profess that snare drums of indefinite pitch should indeed be tuned to pitches. When tapping a snare drum lightly, one can hear a definite pitch. Depending on the depth of the shell and the tension of the heads, the pitches heard can range from G to B; however, these definite pitches are never heard in performance.

Those in the "pitch camp" further advise that the snare or bottom head should be tuned to sound a fourth or fifth above the pitch of the batter head. It is their contention that this highly sophisticated level of tuning a drum of indefinite pitch will provide the best level of performance for that instrument. The player can decide to what degree he wishes to carry the tuning process.

The Bass Drum

Bass drums (Fig. 15.14) are used in three different venues; therefore, they come in three different designs. They are all membranophones and adhere to the construction pattern of the snare drum except that they are bigger and have no snare.

Another type of bass drum, referred to as a kick drum, is used as part of a dance band or "trap" set of drums. This bass drum is constructed in the same pattern as the others, is played with a beater connected to a pedal (Fig. 15.15), and again can vary in size.

A third type of bass drum is used for marching bands. It is lighter in construction, fitted with a harness or carrying device of some kind (Fig. 15.16), and at times is tuned and used in college and show marching bands. These bass drums are also constructed and tuned as are those mentioned above.

Figure 15.14.   Bass drum.

The largest bass drum is used for concert bands or symphonic orchestras. These range in diameter from thirty-two to forty inches with an average depth of about twenty inches. The sizes can vary significantly depending on the desires and needs of the individual situations for which they are to be used.

Figure 15.15.   Bass drum pedal.

Figure 15.16.   Marching bass drum harness.

Cymbals

Cymbals are used to enhance and color music of every type. They can produce an endless variety of effects depending on their design, the material from which they are made, and the process by which they are manufactured.

A cymbal is circular in shape and has a hole in its center for mounting on a stand or for installing a handle used to carry the cymbal. The center area of the cymbal where the hole is located is raised to form a cup shape called the bell (Fig. 15.17A). When struck, the bell section produces a sharp, penetrating sound with short duration.

The larger section beyond the bell, called the bow, has two strike areas. The section closer to the bell is called the ride area (Fig. 15.17B) and, because of its thickness, offers a bolder sound. As the bow tapers out to the thinner section called the crash area (Fig 15.17C), the sound becomes richer and self-sustaining.

Cymbals are categorized by their size and weight because these two factors affect the quality and strength of the sound they produce. Larger and heavier cymbals produce louder sounds. Thinner cymbals produce a richer, lower, more sustained sound.

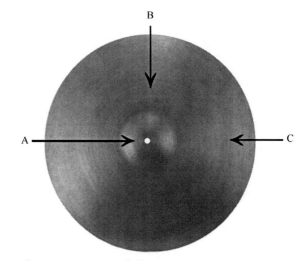

Figure 15.17.   Cymbal parts.

The material from which cymbals are made is generally a type of alloy that is flexible enough to be formed into the shape and density desired by the manufacturer. These are referred to as sheet cymbals because they are formed from sheets of metal. Better quality cymbals are constructed from bell bronze and are forged or hand hammered.

As is the case with many of the percussion instruments, the number of types of cymbals and variations of those types is endless. The following list of named types can act as an introduction to further investigation into the variations of each should that information be relevant to a work under consideration for performance.

There are cymbals called bell, china, clash, crash, hi-hat, ride, sizzle, splash, swish, orchestra, suspended, marching, and finger, just to mention some. These all have a saga of evolution, design, material, and use that can fill volumes.

Timpani

Timpani, timpano in the singular, are definite-pitched instruments. They share many of the structural characteristics of the other drums but with a more sophisticated technology. Timpani are built on a copper, brass, or fiberglass shell shaped like a kettle and thereby comes the nickname kettle drum (Fig. 15.18). The kettle is fitted into a frame, which often has two wheels to facilitate transportation. Also fitted to that frame is a pedal used to make quick adjustments in pitch to the heads.

Timpani Sizes

Timpani are made with bowl sizes ranging from twenty to thirty-two inches in diameter. As is the case with all musical instruments, the larger the instrument the lower the pitch. Larger bowl timpani have lower pitch.

A full classical orchestra or concert band will usually have at least two timpani and as many as five when the score calls for them. Using more than one instrument provides the performer with instant access to a greater variety of tuned timpani sounds. With two timpani tuned a fifth apart and a pedal spread of a fourth (to be explained below), a timpanist is able to play a chromatic scale.

Various sizes of timpani exist to provide a range of notes usually from C2, second line below the staff in the bass clef, to D5, a step above middle C. Older-model instrument sizes can

Figure 15.18. Timpani.

run from twenty to thirty inches in diameter in one-inch increments. In 1978 the industry began to standardize the sizes from twenty to thirty-two inches in three-inch increments.

Tuning the Timpani

Timpani are definite-pitched instruments and have two levels of tuning. There is a fundamental tuning where, with the pedal in the heel down position, the heads are tuned to a particular pitch prescribed by the size of the timpani and the music to be played. The tuning process is identical to that of the snare and bass drums except that the ultimate goal is to achieve the pitch prescribed.

The player taps the head lightly with a timpani mallet about four inches from the rim while turning the tension rod in the direction required to achieve the desired pitch. Again the player alternates the tension rod being turned, as described above, using the 1–4, 2–5, 3–6 pattern.

The following is a list of the notes to which the different size timpani can be tuned and the approximate ascending range of notes that can be produced with the use of the pedal.

A thirty-inch to thirty-two-inch kettle can be tuned to C2 and pedaled up to F3.

A twenty-eight-inch to twenty-nine-inch kettle can be tuned to F3 and pedaled up to D4.

A twenty-five-inch to twenty-six-inch kettle can be tuned to Bb3 and pedaled up to Gb4.

A twenty-three-inch to twenty-four-inch kettle can be tuned to D3 and pedaled up to Bb4.

A twenty-inch to twenty-two-inch kettle can be tuned to F4 and pedaled up to D5.

The Timpani Pedal

Timpani, as definite-pitched instruments, are used to produce a variety of pitches throughout a performance. To facilitate this process, a pedal mechanism is installed in the instrument allowing the timpanist to immediately change pitches within certain parameters without having to go through the tension rod turning process described previously.

Figure 15.19 shows a front view of a timpano with the pedal facing forward, a side view of a timpano with the pedal at the bottom left, and adjacent to those pictures, a diagram of the pedal and its inner spring action.

When the pedal is depressed, the upper cables, which are inside the shell of the drum, pull down on the rim to tighten the head. When this tightening occurs, the pitch is raised in a glissando to an interval of approximately a fifth above the fundamental tone. The player can stop the pedal at any point when the pitch desired is reached.

The timpani pedal must be properly adjusted in order to hold the position set by

Figure 15.19. Timpani pedals.

the player. To adjust the tension of the pedal, proceed as follows:

1. With the head properly tuned to the fundamental tone prescribed, depress the pedal toe down to its maximum position and release the foot from the pedal. It should remain in that position.
2. If the pedal moves back on its own, turn the adjustment knob (visible in the side view tympanum in Figure 15.19) to the right to tighten the tension spring.
3. Conversely, if the pedal in the heel down position moves up on its own, turn the knob to the left to loosen the spring tension.
4. A properly adjusted pedal should remain at any point in its range without having to be held in place by the player's foot.

Timpani Heads

When replacing a timpano head, one will discover that the size of the diameter of the original head, when measured in inches, does not match the size of the instrument. A twenty-six-inch drum does not use a twenty-six-inch head. Timpani heads generally need to be as much as one to two inches larger than the actual circumference of the drum in order to tune properly. The inconsistency in this oversizing of ranging from one to two inches is the result of the individualized size and design evolution of these instruments until they were standardized by the industry in 1978.

To replace a timpano head, it is best to remove the original head and use it as a guide to order the new one. Timpani head charts are provided by the larger drum head manufacturers to help in selecting the proper size.

Timpani Mallets

The mallets used to play the timpani are constructed in the same design as those of other percussion instruments. They consist of a stick or shaft made of wood or a man-made product to which a head is attached. The head can be made of almost anything from soft material, such as cotton or felt, to wood.

The choice of the mallets to be used is entirely up to the performer, the requirements of the music to be played, and the wishes of the music director. It is not uncommon for a timpanist to own a large variety of mallets of all strengths, head densities, and different shaft materials in order to be prepared for all possible music requirements. Figure 15.20 shows just a few of the possible timpani mallet heads available.

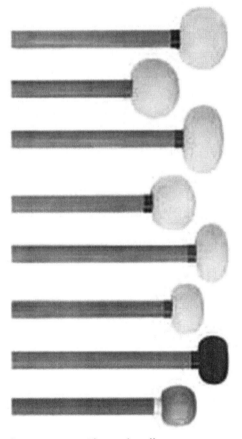

Figure 15.20. Timpani mallets.

Drum Sticks

Drum sticks are made in a variety of sizes and of hardwoods such as oak, hickory, or maple. Aluminum and various forms of plastic, fiberglass, and carbon fiber are also used to make these sticks.

A drum stick (Fig. 15.21) is usually about one and a quarter inches in diameter and around fourteen inches long. The sticks come in such a wide range of sizes, thicknesses, densities, and weights that any effort to categorize them would be futile. Selecting a stick is highly individual and the choice should be left to the player.

There is a labeling system for drum sticks in the music industry, which uses a combination of numbers and letters to identify stick sizes. Unfortunately, this system is far from standardized. Many manufacturers use their own proprietary labeling, which adds to the confusion. This being the case, this manual will by necessity offer guidance in stick selection only in the most general sense.

The three most common size markings that enjoy a reasonable degree of accuracy are 7A, which is thin and light; 5A, which is a bit heavier and most often used for beginners; and 5B, the heaviest of the three, used for big bands and rock music. Any effort for more specific guidance would lack validity and be nonproductive.

The feel of a drum stick in a player's hands has a significant effect on his performance; therefore, careful selection of a stick most suited to the player and the music being performed is essential. The three factors to consider in selection are the strength, weight, and density of the stick.

Because there are so many variations of these design factors, it is recommended that a teacher make the initial selection. As the student progresses, he can then experiment with an assortment of stick sizes to arrive at the one most appropriate for that student and the type of music being performed.

Oak sticks are the heaviest and strongest due to the density of the wood. The strength will provide durability and a strong contact with the strike for the player, and the weight will produce a strong sound. Hickory is more commonly used because of its strength and lighter weight. It is believed by some that hickory sticks produce a better percussion sound than other woods or materials. Maple is the lightest wood used for sticks and, therefore, may be best to produce a quick, light, percussive effect. Rosewood is a very dense

TIP   SHAFT   BUTT

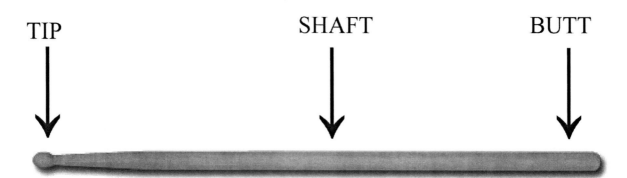

Figure 15.21.   Drum stick.

wood offering durability and a heavier product. Rosewood is the most expensive wood in common use for drum sticks.

There are numerous synthetic products used to make sticks. These are usually more durable than wood and offer an unlimited variety of ways to satisfy the needs of drummers with different "feels" to their sticks.

One additional consideration in selecting a drum stick should be the tip of the stick. Tips are either a continuation of the wood from which the stick is made or are made of nylon and added on to the stick. Nylon tips produce a crisp sound and are particularly effective on cymbals whereas wooden tips produce a warmer, more subtle sound. Also

available are rubber tips (Fig. 15.22), which can slip over the original tip and are useful for practice when a drum is not available or when little sound is desired.

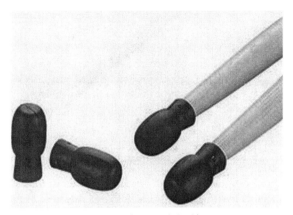

Figure 15.22.   Snare drum stick tips.

Drum Mallets

Drum mallets are sticks or shafts with a bulbous head on one or both ends. The head can be made of almost anything from metal to soft wrapped cotton and can be any degree of hardness depending on the intended use of the mallet.

Bass drum mallets are often called beaters. Their heads (Fig. 15.23) can be made of wood or cotton depending on the degree of hardness required for the music being played. These beaters also come with a double head, or a head on each end of the stick (Fig. 15.24). The two heads are usually different sizes and can be of different hardness.

Two-headed beaters permit the player to quickly change the quality of the sound by using one head or the other. They can also be used to produce a bass drum roll by the player holding the beater in the center of the shaft and rapidly rotating the wrist from left to right.

Figure 15.23.   Bass drum beaters.

Mallets used for tuned instruments with bars that must be struck to produce sound, such as orchestra bells, the glockenspiel, or the xylophone, require a hard-headed mallet. These can be made of wood, nylon, metal, or hard rubber (Fig. 15.25). Other tuned instruments that produce a less percussive sound,

Figure 15.24.   Double-headed bass drum beater.

Figure 15.25.   Hard-headed mallets.

such as the vibraphone, use softer mallets. Soft mallets have a hard core that is wrapped with a softer material like cotton, nylon, yarn, or other forms of corded fabric (Fig. 15.26).

The shafts and heads of mallets are made of a variety of materials. The heads can be made of anything from the softest materials to steel depending on the type of sound desired and the instrument for which its use is intended. The choice must be made by the performer and the demands of the music being performed. The shafts can be made of various types of wood or plastic or other man-made material.

Figure 15.26.   Soft-headed mallets.

Brushes

Brushes (Fig. 15.27) are used for special effects on snare drums and cymbals. Metal bristles are connected to a rigid wire, which is fed through a hollow handle. The wire has a loop on the end, which is used to pull and draw the bristles into the handle. When the wire is pushed into the handle, the bristles fan out and the brushes are ready for use. In this manner, the player can adjust the spread and flexibility of the brushes to achieve different effects, and then collapse the brushes for easy transportation.

Figure 15.27.   Brushes.

The Drum Set

A drum set, sometimes referred to as a trap set or drum kit, can vary in size depending on its intended use and the budget of its owner. A three-piece set would consist of a snare drum, bass drum and floor tom, a ride cymbal, crash cymbal, and a hi-hat cymbal. Cymbals are not included in the count of a trap set.

Adding two side or mounted toms would result in a five-piece set providing the player greater performance versatility (Fig. 15.28). These additions require appropriate stands and hardware, and the set should include a throne for the drummer (Fig. 15.29).

Figure 15.29.   Drummer's throne.

Figure 15.28.   Drum set.

The hi-hat cymbal (Fig. 15.30) and bass drum are activated with a pedal (Fig. 15.31) while the drummer plays with both hands.

Figure 15.31.   Bass drum pedal.

Figure 15.30.   Hi-hat cymbal.

Smaller Percussion Instruments

An array of smaller instruments are available that can be added to a set to extend its versatil-ity. Among the most common are the triangle, wood block, and cow bell (Fig. 15.32).

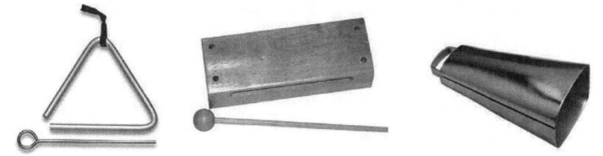

Figure 15.32.   Small percussion instruments: triangle (left), wood block (middle), and cow bell (right).

The Electric Drum

With the evolution of the electronic syn-thesizer, the drum industry has been able to develop a product that can produce a variety of prescribed percussion sounds. Pads with a resilient drum head–like surface contain a sensor that, when struck, sends an electric impulse through a cable or midi connection to a sound-producing and amplifying system. The individual pads can be designed and pro-grammed to replicate various types of drum, cymbal, or other percussion sounds. Different-sized pads are set up on stands in the same configuration as a trap set so the player can experience the drumming process as he would on an acoustic drum set (Fig. 15.33).

The extraordinary flexibility of this appa-ratus allows a performer to produce an infinite assortment of sounds duplicating both tuned and non-tuned percussion instruments. The set can be used with full amplification for a re-alistic percussion sound or it can be used with earphones for practice with very little sound audible to the surrounding environment. An-other advantage to this setup when compared

Figure 15.33.   Electric drum.

to a traditional acoustic drum set is the ease of portability and storage the former offers.

These devices do have a level of contrived sound that can only be judged acceptable or not by the player and the circumstance in which the set is to be used. Additionally, the feel of the set to the drummer, although closely resembling that of a traditional mem-branophone, does fall a bit short.

Practice Pads

Practice pads were conceived of as a way to provide a student or drummer with a piece of equipment on which to practice that would be mobile, inexpensive, quiet, and yet have the feel of a drum or set of drums. The music industry has responded with a variety of contrivances called practice pads. They range from a wooden square with a rubber pad attached, to a complete set of circular pads with surfaces that in some way will respond with the feel of a drum without producing much sound.

Since there are so many different types of practice pads available, and all with their individual attributes, these pads are best identified by the manufacturer's brand name. Figure 15.34 shows a few of the most commonly used of the many available. It is best for an individual who is seeking one of these devices to go to a large, well stocked music store and try each one on display.

Wooden Square with Rubber Pad

Remo - Has a coated plastic batter head

Gladstone - Solid rubber fits on the head of a snare drum or can be used on any surface

Gibraltar GP08 - Rack Practice Kit
Many options available to create an individualized set up

DW Go Anywhere Practice Set
Claims excellent feel and rebound

Evans two-sided speed workout drum pad Gum rubber side for speed and a neoprene surface for workout practice

Remo Practice Pad Set – An assortment of different size pads with coated drum heads intended to produce a live drum feel.

Figure 15.34.   Drum pads.

Mallet Instruments

Mallet instruments are named so because they are played by being struck with some type of mallet (Fig. 15.35). The mallets used have heads that are graduated in hardness to the degree needed to produce the percussive effect desired. The material from which the heads are made can range from a soft cotton to denser cotton, felt, wood, plastic, or steel.

The Xylophone

The xylophone (Fig. 15.36) is the most common instrument in the mallet percussion

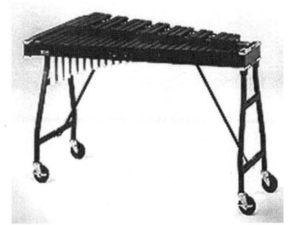

Figure 15.36.   Xylophone.

Figure 15.35.   Assorted mallets.

family. The instrument is designed with tuned wooden or synthetic material bars in the form of a piano keyboard. When struck with a mallet, these bars respond idiophonically (i.e., vibrating in their totality).

Two mallets, one for each hand, with heads of the density appropriate for the music to be played, are used to strike the bars. Usually the mallets used have heads of a hard plastic, acrylic, or hard rubber, but, depending on the effect to be achieved, softer core, cotton-wrapped mallets change the effect to a more mellow sound. Four mallets can also be used, two in each hand, to perform music requiring this technique.

Xylophone bars produce a bright but not a long, sustained sound. To increase the duration of the sound, some are built with tubes or resonators under the bars, which sustain the otherwise shorter sound the bar alone would produce.

Xylophones are transposing instruments with the notes sounding one octave above the written note. The range of the instrument generally starts at F3 (below middle C) and, depending on the instrument model, can extend up from two and a half octaves to as much as four octaves.

The Marimba

The marimba (Fig. 15.37) may be considered to be one of the solo instruments in the percussion family. It is designed with wooden bars in the form of a piano keyboard and is generally played with four moderate to soft-headed mallets. The marimba produces a rich, warm sound that is less percussive than that of the xylophone.

The mellow sound is attributed to the fact that the bars are made of wood and that each bar is fitted with a tube-shaped resonator

Figure 15.37.   Marimba.

hanging below. The tubes are graduated in size and modified in shape to accommodate the pitch of the bar it services. When the bars are struck, the vibrations they produce travel down into the resonators. These act as amplifiers of the sound much as a violin body amplifies the vibrations of its strings.

Depending on the size of the instrument, marimbas have a range of between four and five octaves, the lowest note being C3, the second being space C in the bass clef, and the highest being four to five octaves above.

The Vibraphone

The vibraphone (Fig. 15.38) is the most sophisticated of the mallet instruments. It has the same piano-like keyboard as that of the

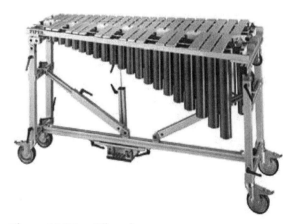

Figure 15.38.   Vibraphone.

xylophone and the marimba except that the bars on the vibraphone are made of aluminum instead of wood or a man-made material. Due to this difference, a note struck on a vibraphone will sustain much longer than one on the other mallet instruments.

To control the sustaining sound, vibraphones are equipped with a damper system operated by a pedal much like that of a piano pedal. When the pedal is depressed, felt pads that are in contact with the sound bars are released and the bars are free to vibrate. When the pedal is released, the pads resume contact and the vibration is stopped.

Vibraphones are equipped with resonators, which are metal tubes open at the top and closed at the bottom. These tubes contain discs run by a motor or, in the more sophisticated models, controlled by a computer. The discs rotate within the resonator resulting in the unique vibraphone sound. There is a resonator under each bar.

When a bar is struck, the vibrations from the bar travel down the tube-shaped resonator to the closed bottom and then bounce back up to the bar only to repeat the process. This action increases the intensity of the fundamental within the note, producing the vibraphone sound.

The range of most vibraphones extends from F3 (F below middle C) to F6, or about three octaves up. Larger, more expensive models are expanded by as much as an additional octave going from C3, an octave below middle C, to C7.

Vibraphones use an electric adjustable speed motor and pulley assembly mounted on one side of the instrument to drive the discs in the resonators. The more advanced models have motors that are computerized to provide greater control over the discs in the resonators.

The basic mallets used to play a vibraphone have a slim, hardwood or plastic shaft with a head of hard rubber wrapped with a soft cotton or synthetic cord. Because the density and resilience of the mallet head has a profound effect on the quality and timbre of the sound produced, players generally keep a wide variety of mallets in their quiver. By doing so, the players have the ability to produce any type of sound—from piercing and metallic to amorous and mellifluous.

One extraordinary, albeit seldom used, sound-generating process replacing mallet use on a vibraphone is the use of a cello or double bass bow. When drawn along the edge of the bar, the percussive character of the sound generated is turned into a smoother, purer tone.

The Glockenspiel

The glockenspiel is among the smaller, more mobile of the tuned mallet instruments. It comes in two configurations both played with the same technique and producing the same sound. The bell lyre-shaped glockenspiel (Fig. 15.39) is easily carried with the use of a harness for marching situations or can be placed on a stand for stage performances. The encased glockenspiel (Fig. 15.40) is best used for stage performances for obvious reasons.

The bars of the glockenspiel, like other tuned mallet instruments, are configured as a piano keyboard. Played using nylon, metal, or other hard-tipped mallets, the sound produced is very bright and well sustained. It is, therefore, sometimes necessary to moderate the enthusiasm of the performer to meet the requirements of the music being performed.

Glockenspiels are tuned in the key of C, have a range of about two and a half octaves, and transpose at the octave, sounding an

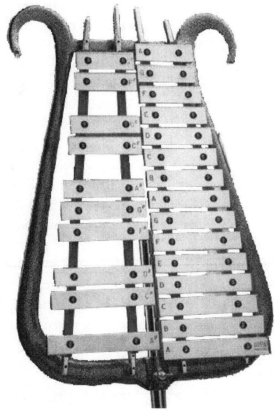

Figure 15.39.   Marching glockenspiel.

Figure 15.40.   Encased glockenspiel.

octave above the written note. Music written for the instrument generally ranges from G3, a fourth below middle C, to C6, two octaves above middle C.

Chimes and Tubular Bells

Chimes, also called tubular bells (Fig. 15.41), are mallet instruments that, because of their expanded overtone series (see chapter 1 of this manual), produce a church bell–like sound. A set of chimes is constructed of hollow metal tubes usually about one and a quarter to one and a half inches in diameter. These are graduated in size and tuned to definite pitches in a chromatic sequence. The tubes have a cap on the top, which is used as the strike point for the mallet. Suspended on a frame and held by wire, gut, or other chord-like products, the tubes are free to vibrate when struck.

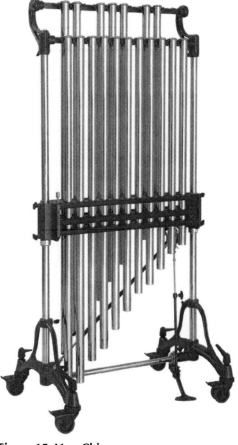

Figure 15.41.   Chimes.

The range of a set of chimes is usually one and a half octaves starting from C4, to middle C, and up an octave and a half to F6. The tubes are arranged chromatically in the piano keyboard pattern.

The tubular construction of the chimes produces a sustained tone controlled by a dampening system, which the player activates by pressing a pedal. When the pedal is depressed, all tubes are dampened. Dampening single tubes is done by hand.

Summary

Percussion instruments can be likened to the spices in a fine meal. The meal can be prepared and eaten without spices but is exponentially better with them. Such is the relationship of music to percussion instruments from the smallest triangle to an entire six-piece section of timpani.

When listening to classical music, an audience is less inclined to notice the important role the cymbal, bass drum, snare drum, or triangle has in enriching the music. It is the string, brass, or woodwind sections that get almost all the credit. Such is also the case with any prepared food. The food is recognized by its main ingredient and not by its condiments. Leave out the condiments and their absence will be noted. Omit the percussion section from a performance and the result will be the same.

This situation is rarely the case in many of the current rock or heavy metal bands, for those groups often center on an elaborate multi-piece trap set of drums. There the drummer is more likely to get his or her due.

Chapter 16

Conclusion

The complexity of music composition, performance, and musical instrument technology is a non-issue in the minds of most who are not directly involved in the field. We on the inside know better. The knowledge, imagination, and skill required to design and build a good, functioning instrument is beyond comprehension to most. Additionally, to produce a stellar performance on one of these instruments requires that the performer commits a lifetime to achieving that goal. And that commitment would be to one instrument. This being the case, when we mere mortals are required to deal with musical instruments on which we have *not* achieved excellence, we are confronted with all of the challenges that the specialists strive to overcome but with neither the time nor the background to give ourselves a jump start on the new-to-us instrument.

This manual reduces this challenge by introducing the more popular acoustical musical instruments currently in general use to those who must deal with a non-major instrument. The topics covered and the depth to which they were pursued were selected based on a determination of the most probable needs of a trained musical instrument practitioner who is confronted with the task of dealing with an instrument with which she is not proficient.

Let it be noted that for every topic covered, there exists an almost incalculable quantity of additional information available beyond the basic fundamentals presented in this manual. An example of this phenomenon can be found in fingering charts for woodwind instruments. This book offers basic fingering charts for the five most commonly used woodwind instruments. More advanced charts can be found offering alternate fingerings, which can number two or three fingerings for one note. Then there is the matter of trill fingerings for most notes in an instrument's range.

Embouchure and tone production are topics that have enjoyed unending attention and commentary by musical cognoscienti. Smile, don't smile, soft reed, hard reed, 7C, 3A, deep cup, shallow cup, light stick, heavy stick, and so forth. Who is right and who is wrong? The only rational conclusion this writer has come to after a lifetime of listening and trying is that much depends on the individual performer and the music to be performed.

Almost all opinions in these areas can result in very effective solutions in certain situations. Oral configuration, muscle tone, respiratory capacity, physical endurance, and whatever other physical and emotional characteristics involved in producing a tone on an instrument are all factors that contribute to the success of the final product. It's all individual.

The Musical Instrument Desk Reference will assist you in getting a quick start on any of the instruments covered. You have shown great wisdom in acquiring this manual. It will serve you well.

Index

About the Author

Michael Pagliaro is certified by the New York State Department of Education as a Teacher of Music (grades K–12), Supervisor of Secondary Education, and Secondary School Principal, as well as by the New York City Board of Education as Teacher of Orchestral Music. He holds the degrees of BS in Music, MA in Music Education, and ScD in Musical Instrument Technology.

He has devoted more than five decades to teaching the technology and science of acoustical orchestral instruments to music teachers, students, technicians, supervisors, and professionals in the field. In addition, he has filled the role of military band master, church choir director, founder of two musical instrument companies still in operation, patent holder and inventor of four music-related products sold worldwide, and has written four books and nineteen articles on musical instruments and music in general.

The Musical Instrument Desk Reference: A Guide to How Band and Orchestral Instruments Work was written in response to requests from practitioners who, for whatever reason, are required to deal with instruments on which they are not proficient. Many chapters contain both an easy-reference quick start followed by an expanded, in-depth study, providing important information on woodwind, brass, non-fretted string, and percussion instruments commonly used in concert band and orchestras.

CPSIA information can be obtained at www.ICGtesting.com
Printed in the USA
BVOW051731070113

309764BV00004B/13/P